I0008352

Contents

1.0 OPERATORS AND SPECIAL CHARACTERS

The commonly used **MATLAB** operators and special characters used to solve many engineering and science problems are given below.

Operators and Special Characters:

+ ....plus
- ....minus
* ....matrix multiplication
.* ....array multiplication
^ ....matrix power
.^ ....array power
\ ....backslash (left division)
/ ....slash (right division)
. / and. \ ....right and left array division
: ....colon
( ).......................... parentheses
[ ].......................... brackets
{ }.......................... curly braces
... . continuation
, comma
; ....semicolon
. ... decimal point
!.......................... exclamation point
'................... transpose and quote
.' .... non-conjugated transpose

=................... assignment
==................. equality
< >................. relational operators
&................. logical **AND**
|................... logical OR
xor............... logical exclusive OR
~................... logical NOT

1.1 Plot of active and reactive powers with respect to the power angle as constant (i.e. not in radians)

>> teta=0:10:90;

>> E=415;V=300;X=0.03;

>> P=(3*V*E./X)*sin(teta);

>> Q=(3*V*E./X)*cos(teta)-(3*V*V./X);

>> plot(teta,P);grid on

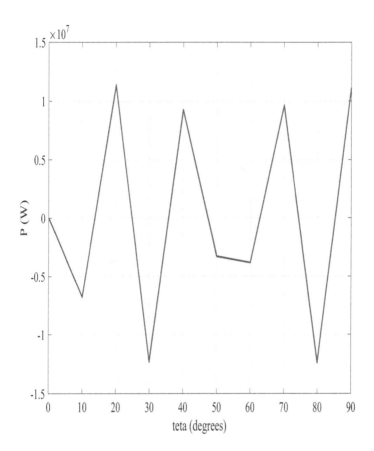

>> plot(x,y,'r');grid on

Click on the EDIT, scroll down and click on
FIGURE PROPERTIES. You can now edit the
graph as you desire. Then

>> x=-10:1:10;

>> y=x.^2+5.*x+6;

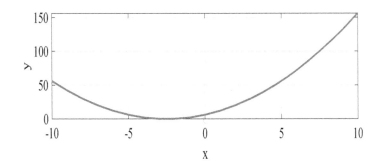

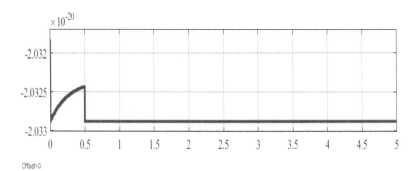

Offset=0

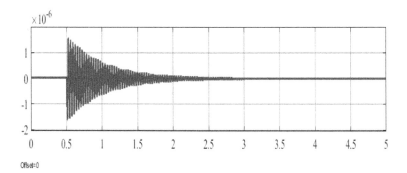

Offset=0

8

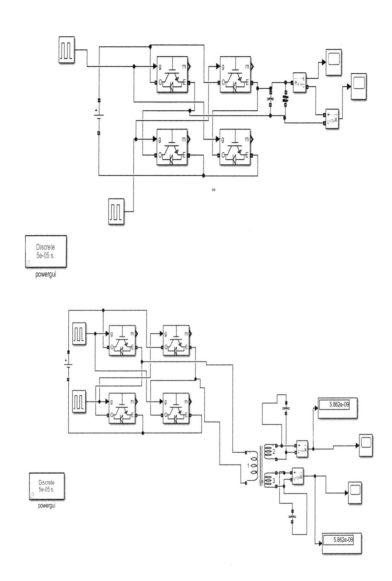

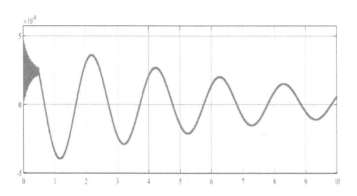

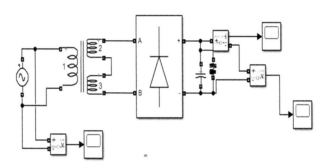

Discrete
5e-05 s.

powergui

10

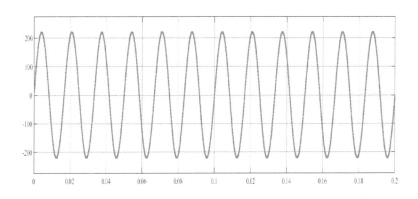

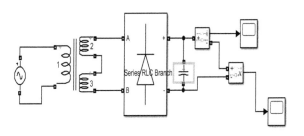

Continuous

powergui

11

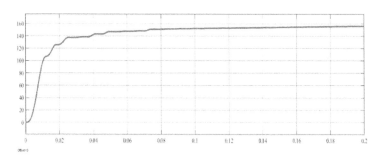

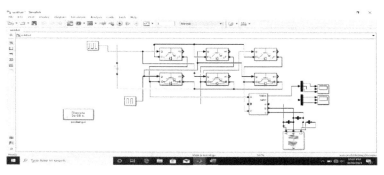

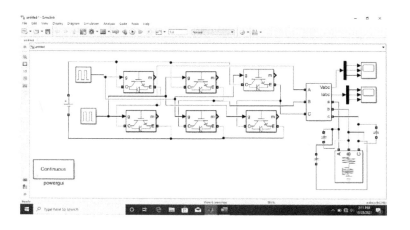

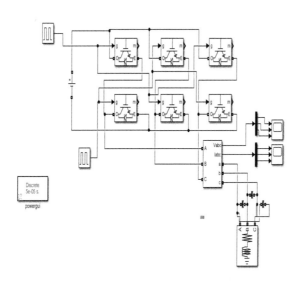

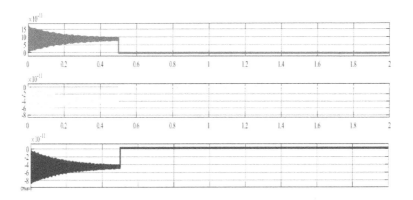

13

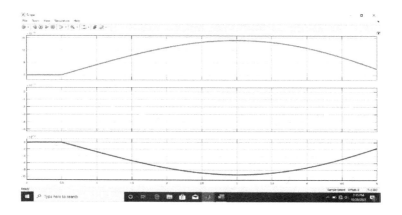

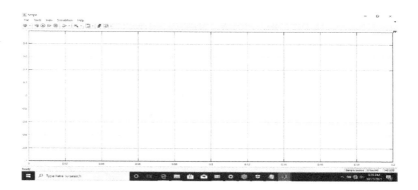

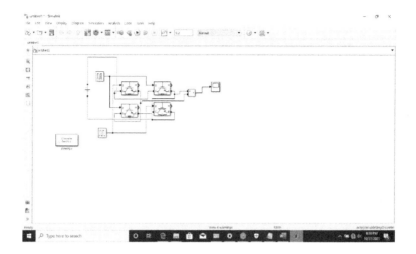

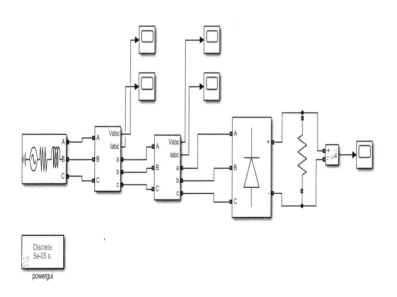

Discrete
5e-05 s.

powergui

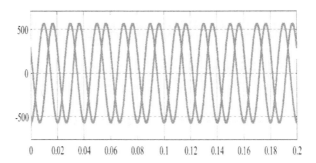

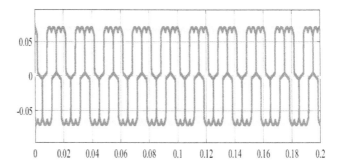

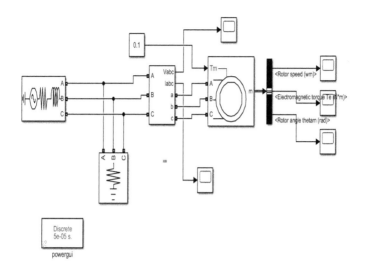

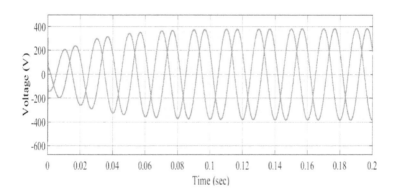

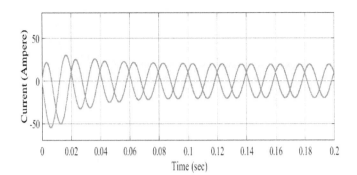

Offset=0

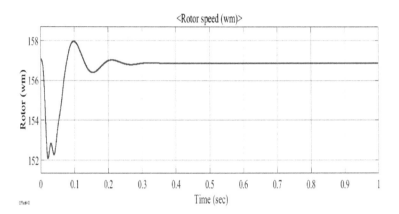

Offset=0

1.2 Steps to be taken to get the FFT Analysis
Step 1

Click on the *scope* to display the graph then click on *view*

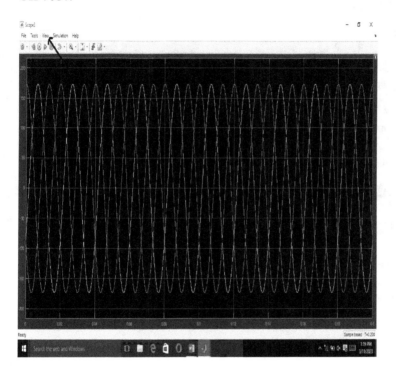

Step 2

Scroll to *configuration properties* and click on it

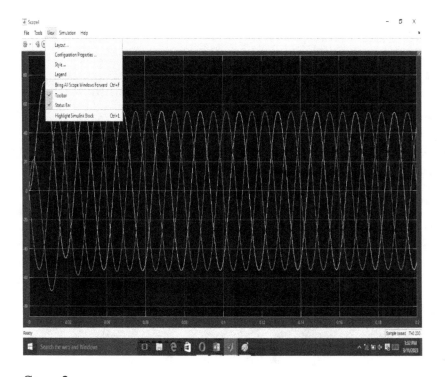

Step 3

Scroll to *logging* and click on *log data to workspace*

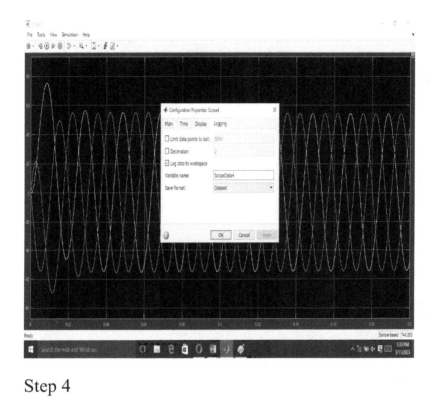

Step 4

Click on *powergui* (make sure is on discrete).
Scroll to tools and click on *FFT Analysis*

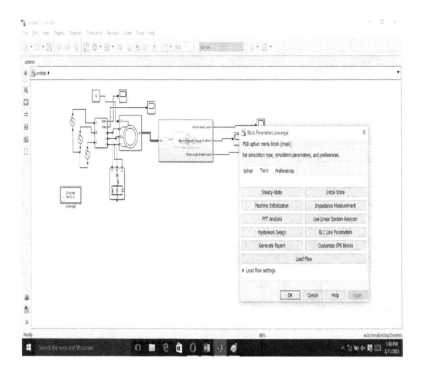

Step 5

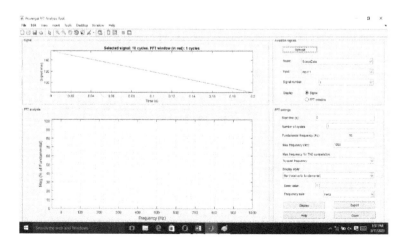

22

Step 6

Simulate the circuit again to display results.

Step 7

Click on **Refresh**. The scope data will be displayed on **name** under **Available signals**

Step 8

Double Click on display to display the FFT Analysis for the respective scope data.

Example

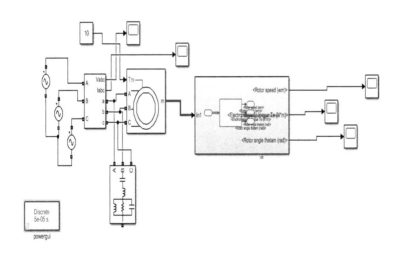

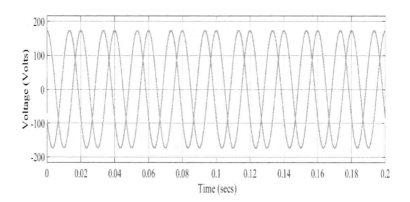

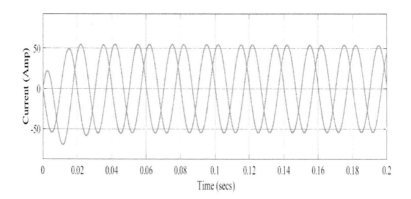

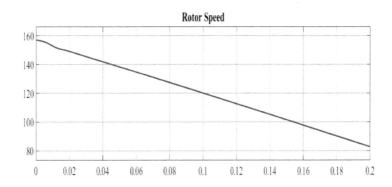

Rotor Speed

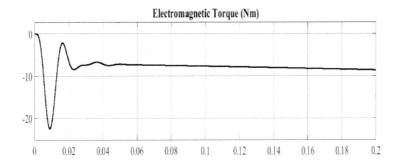

Electromagnetic Torque (Nm)

25

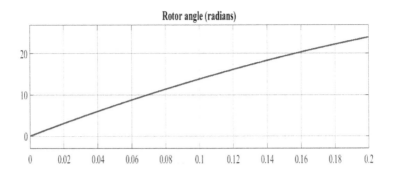

FFT Analysis

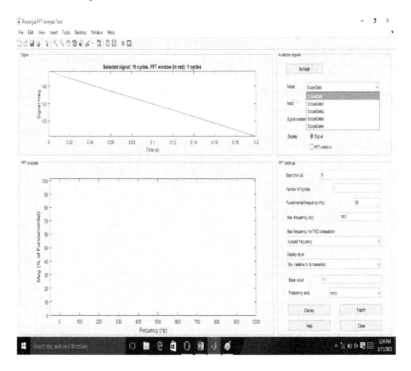

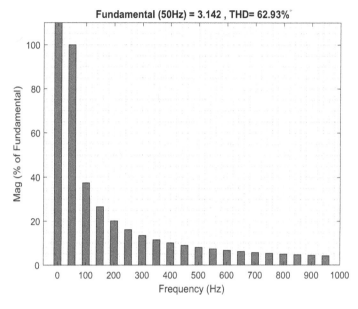

Fundamental (50Hz) = 3.142 , THD= 62.93%

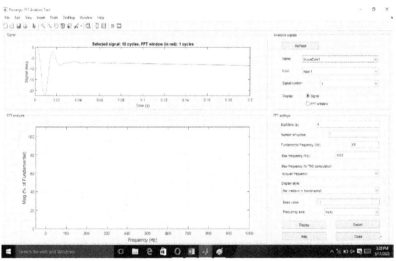

27

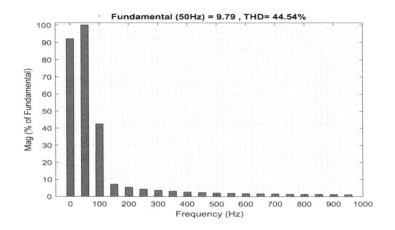

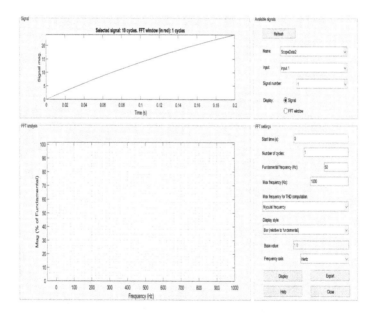

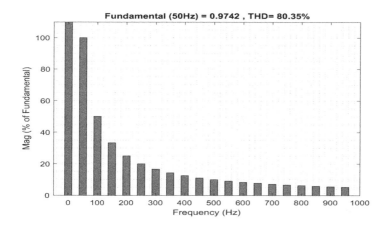

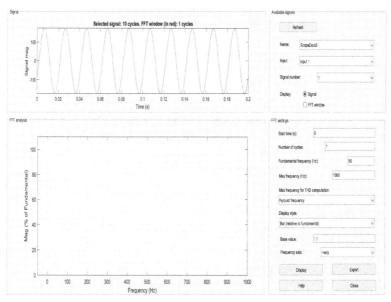

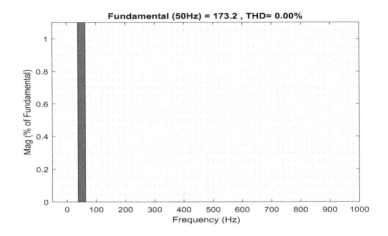

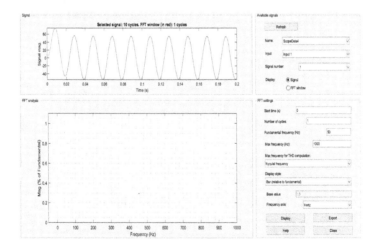

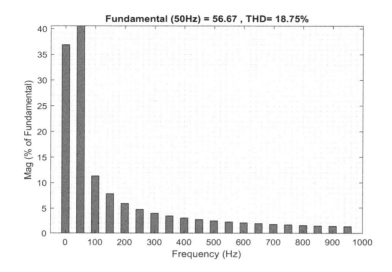

Fundamental (50Hz) = 56.67 , THD= 18.75%

>> teta=0:10:90;

>> E=415;V=300;X=0.03;

>> P=(3*V*E./X)*sin(teta);

>> Q=(3*V*E./X)*cos(teta)-(3*V*V./X);

>> plot(teta,Q);grid on

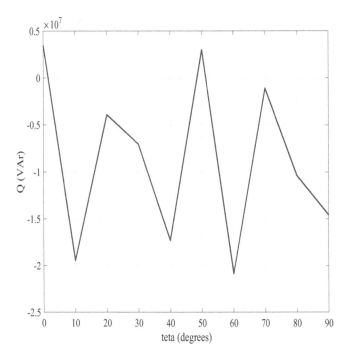

>> teta=0:10:90;

>> E=415;V=300;X=0.03;

>> P=(3*V*E./X)*sin(teta);

>> Q=(3*V*E./X)*cos(teta)-(3*V*V./X);

>> plot(sin(teta),P);grid on

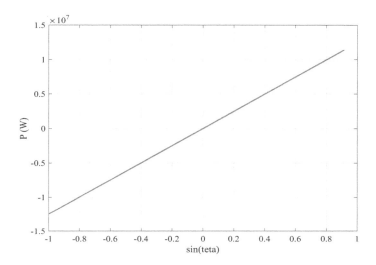

Click on the graph to insert labels and title of the graph. On the x axis it is labeled as *sin(teta)* and y axis as *P(active power)*

>> teta=0:30:150;

>> V=300;X=10;E=415;

>> P=(3*V*E./X)*sin(teta);

>> Q=(3*V*E./X)*cos(teta)-(3*V*V./X);

>> plot(cos(teta),P);grid on

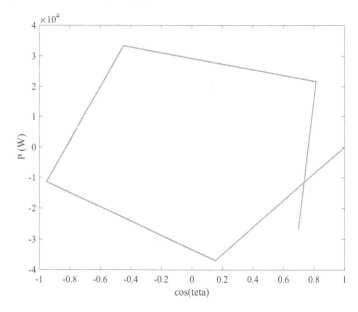

```
>> teta=0:30:150;

>> V=300;X=10;E=415;

>> P=(3*V*E./X)*sin(teta);

>> Q=(3*V*E./X)*cos(teta)-(3*V*V./X);

>> plot(sin(teta),Q);grid on
```

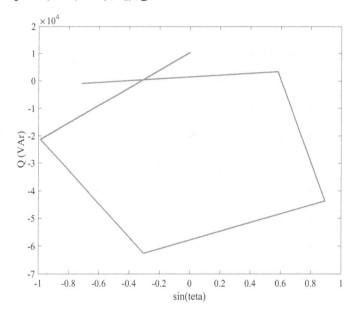

```
>> teta=0:30:150;

>> V=300;X=10;E=415;

>> P=(3*V*E./X)*sin(teta);
```

\>\> Q=(3*V*E./X)*cos(teta)-(3*V*V./X);

\>\> plot(cos(teta),Q);grid on

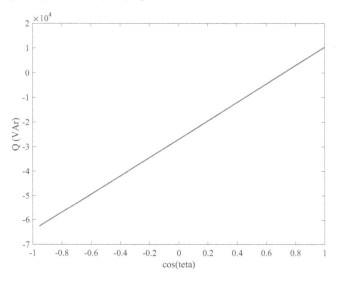

1.3 Plot of active and reactive powers with respect to the power angle measured in radians

\>\> teta=0:pi/18:2*pi;

\>\> E=415;V=300;X=10;

\>\> P=(3*V*E./X)*sin(teta);

>> Q=(3*V*E./X)*cos(teta)-(3*V*V./X);

>> plot(teta,P);grid on

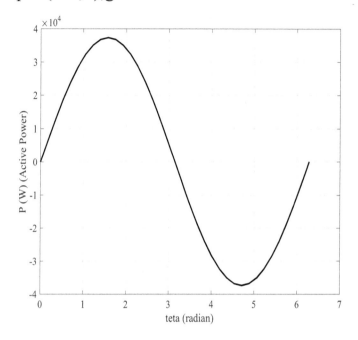

>> teta=0:pi/18:2*pi;

>> E=415;V=300;X=10;

>> P=(3*V*E./X)*sin(teta);

>> Q=(3*V*E./X)*cos(teta)-(3*V*V./X);

>> plot(teta,Q);grid on

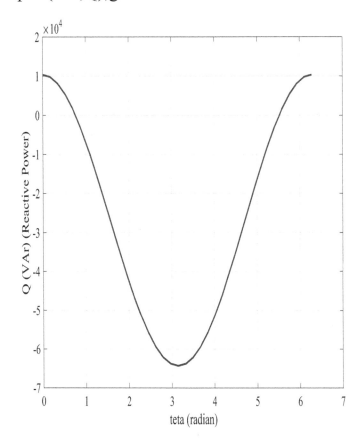

CHAPTER 2

2.0 PLOT OF TRIGONOMETRICAL EQUATION AND POWER RELATED PROBLEMS

```
>> teta=[0:pi/18:2*pi/3];

>> E=415;

>> V=300;

>> X=10;

>> P=(3*V*E./X)*sin(teta);

>> Q=(3*V*E./X)*cos(teta)-(3*V*V./X);

>> plot(teta,P)

>> plot(teta,Q)
```

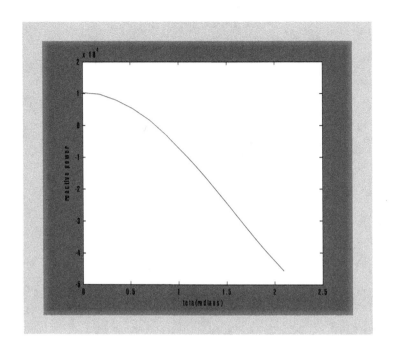

```
>> t=-2*pi:0.1:2*pi;

>> x=10*sin(t);y=10*cos(t);

>> plot(x,y)

>> grid on
```

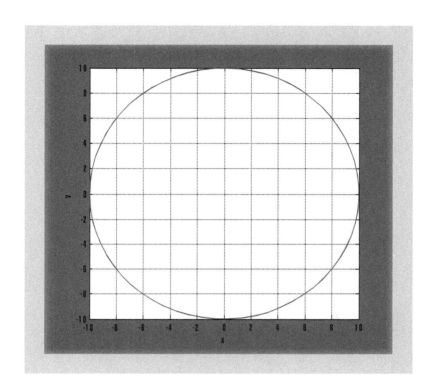

>> t=-2*pi:pi/18:2*pi

t =

Columns 1 through 12

-6.2832   -6.1087   -5.9341   -5.7596   -5.5851   -
5.4105   -5.2360   -5.0615   -4.8869   -4.7124   -
4.5379   -4.3633

Columns 13 through 24

-4.1888   -4.0143   -3.8397   -3.6652   -3.4907   -
3.3161   -3.1416   -2.9671   -2.7925   -2.6180   -
2.4435   -2.2689

Columns 25 through 36

-2.0944   -1.9199   -1.7453   -1.5708   -1.3963   -
1.2217   -1.0472   -0.8727   -0.6981   -0.5236   -
0.3491   -0.1745

Columns 37 through 48

        0   0.1745   0.3491   0.5236   0.6981
0.8727   1.0472   1.2217   1.3963   1.5708
1.7453   1.9199

Columns 49 through 60

    2.0944   2.2689   2.4435   2.6180   2.7925
2.9671   3.1416   3.3161   3.4907   3.6652
3.8397   4.0143

Columns 61 through 72

    4.1888   4.3633   4.5379   4.7124   4.8869
5.0615   5.2360   5.4105   5.5851   5.7596
5.9341   6.1087

Column 73

6.2832

```
>> x=10.*sin(t);

>> y=10.*cos(t);

>> plot(t,x,'r')

>> hold on

>> plot(t,y,'g')

>> hold on

>> plot(x,y,'m')
```

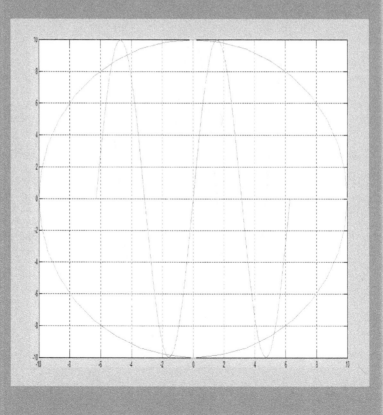

```
>> teta=[0:pi/18:pi];

>> E=415;

>> V=300;

>> X=10;

>> P=(3*V*E./X)*sin(teta);

>> Q=(3*V*E./X)*cos(teta)-(3*V*V./X);

>> plot(teta,P)

>>
```

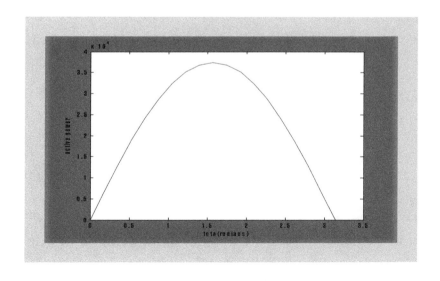

```
>> teta=[0:pi/18:pi];

>> E=415;

>> V=300;

>> X=10;

>> P=(3*V*E./X)*sin(teta);

>> Q=(3*V*E./X)*cos(teta)-(3*V*V./X);

>> plot(teta,P)

>> plot(teta,Q)

>>
```

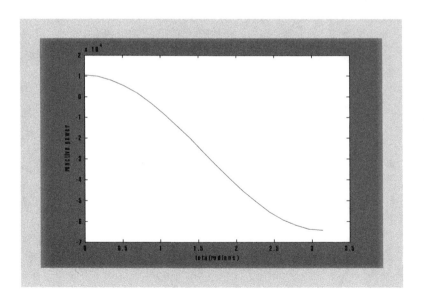

```
>> teta=[0:pi/18:2*pi];

>> E=415;

>> V=300;

>> X=10;

>> P=(3*V*E./X)*sin(teta);

>> Q=(3*V*E./X)*cos(teta)-(3*V*V./X);

>> plot(teta,P)
```

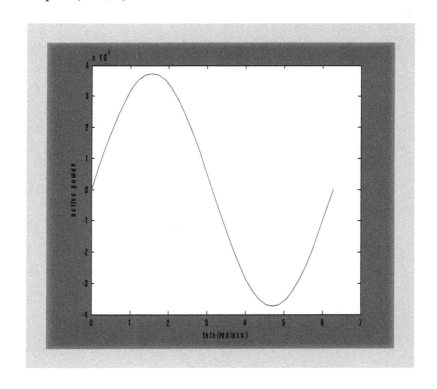

```
>> teta=[0:pi/18:2*pi];

>> E=415;

>> V=300;

>> X=10;

>> P=(3*V*E./X)*sin(teta);

>> Q=(3*V*E./X)*cos(teta)-(3*V*V./X);

>> plot(teta,P)

>> plot(teta,Q)
```

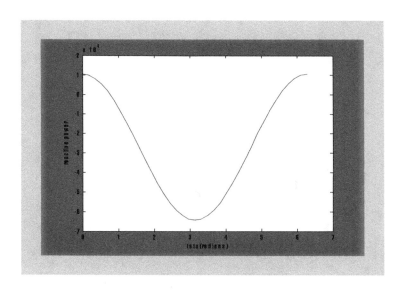

```
>> teta=0:pi/18:2*pi;

>> E=415;

>> V=300;

>> X=10;

>> P=(3*V*E./X)*sin(teta);

>> Q=(3*V*E./X)*cos(teta)-(3*V*V./X);

>> plot(sin(teta),P)

>> grid on
```

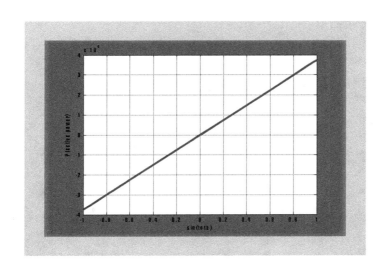

```
>> teta=0:pi/18:2*pi;

>> E=415;

>> V=300;

>> X=10;

>> P=(3*V*E./X)*sin(teta);

>> Q=(3*V*E./X)*cos(teta)-(3*V*V./X);

>> plot(sin(teta),P)

>> grid on

>> plot(cos(teta),P)

>> grid on
```

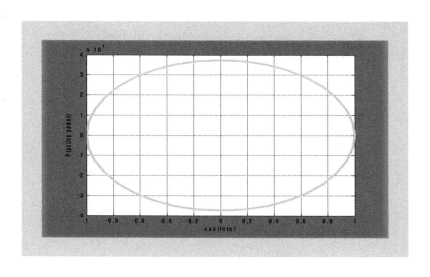

```
>> x=[-pi:pi/18:pi];

>> y=sin(x);

>> f=cos(x);

>> hold on

>> plot(x,y,'r');grid on

>> plot(x,f,'g');grid on
```

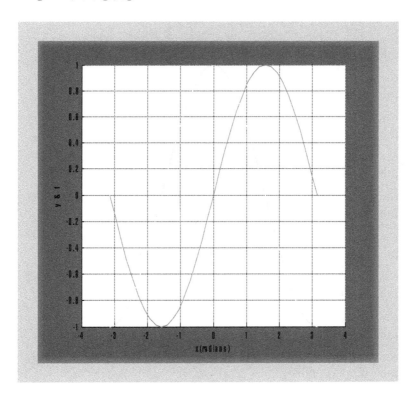

```
>> x=0:pi/18:2*pi;

>> Ir=sin(x);

>> Iy=sin(x+2*pi/3);

>> Ib=sin(x+4*pi/3);

>> hold on

>> plot(x,Ir,'r')

>> plot(x,Iy,'c')

>> plot(x,Ib,'m')

>> grid on
```

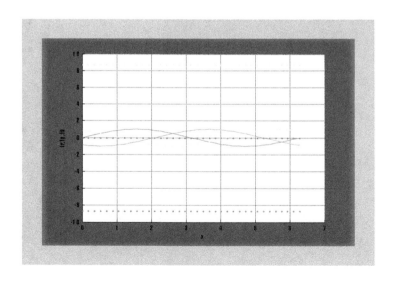

CHAPTER 3

3.0 POWER ANGLE SOLUTION AND AC MACHINE

```
>> teta=0:pi/18:2*pi;

>> E=415;

>> V=300;

>> X=10;

>> P=(3*V*E./X)*sin(teta);

>> Q=(3*V*E./X)*cos(teta)-(3*V*V./X);

>> plot(sin(teta),P)

>> grid on

>> plot(cos(teta),P)

>> grid on

>> plot(sin(teta),Q)

>> grid on

>>
```

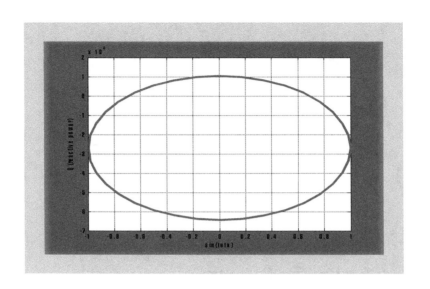

```
>> teta=0:pi/18:2*pi;

>> E=415;

>> V=300;

>> X=10;

>> P=(3*V*E./X)*sin(teta);

>> Q=(3*V*E./X)*cos(teta)-(3*V*V./X);

>> plot(sin(teta),P)

>> grid on

>> plot(cos(teta),P)
```

\>\> grid on

\>\> plot(sin(teta),Q)

\>\> grid on

\>\> plot(cos(teta),Q)

\>\> grid on

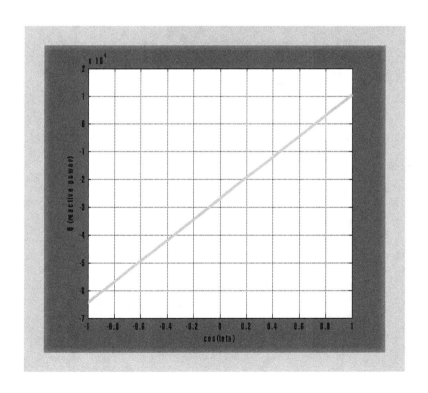

Plot of number of poles against synchronous speed

p=[2:2:12];

>> freq=50;

>> N=120*freq./p;

>> plot(p,N)

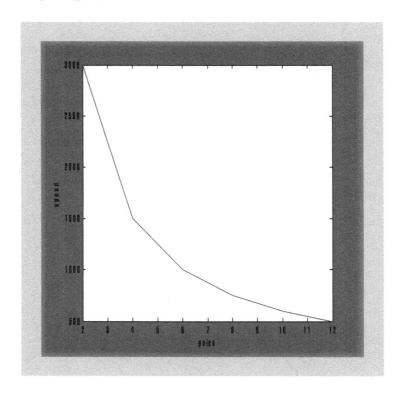

Plot of synchronous speed against torque indicating probable error when entering the codes

> N=[0:20:1500];

>> Pout=3750;

>> T=Pout/(2*3.142*N);

??? Error using ==> mrdivide

Matrix dimensions must agree.

>> T=Pout./(2*3.142*N);

>> plot(N,T)

>> grid on

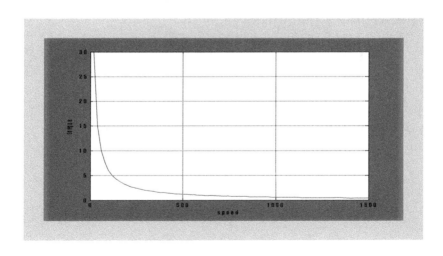

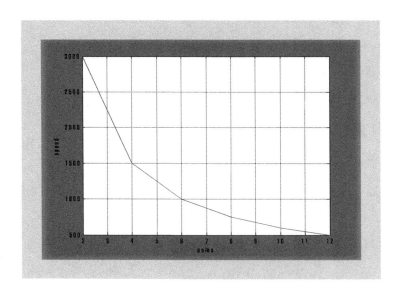

>> n=0:100:3000;

>> P=2250;

>> T=P/(2*pi.*n)

??? Error using ==> mrdivide

Matrix dimensions must agree.

>> T=P./(2*pi*n);

>> plot(n,T,'m');grid on

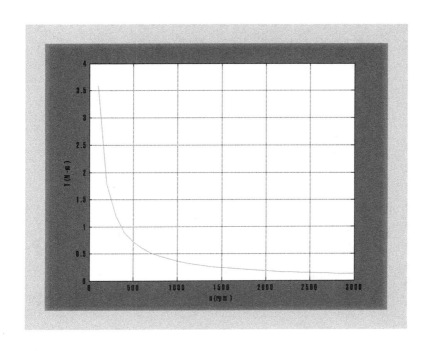

\>> n=[500:50:3000];

\>> p=3750;

\>> t=p./(2*3.142*n);

\>> plot(n,t)

\>> grid on

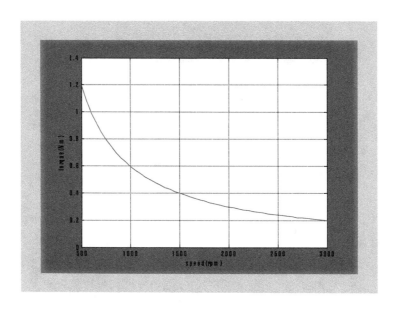

Use of quadratic formula to solve values of $x^2+4x+4=0$

\>> a=1,b=4,c=4

a =

   1

b =

   4

c =

   4

```
>> x1=(-b+sqrt(b.^2-4*a*c))/2*a,x2=(-b-sqrt(b.^2-
4*a*c))/2*a
```

x1 =

 -2

x2 =

 -2

CHAPTER 4

4.0 A METHOD OF PLOTTING THE GRAPH OF QUADRATIC EQUATIONS.

>> syms x

>> ezplot(x.^2+4*x+4,[-10 10])

>> grid on

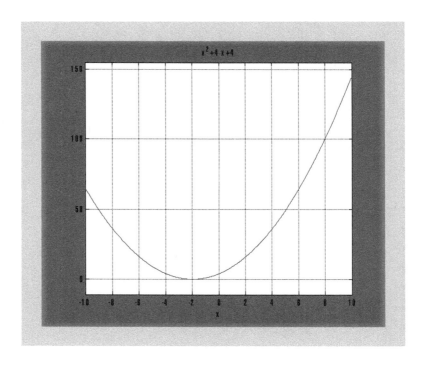

y=x.^2+5.*x+6;

>> syms x

>> ezplot(x.^2+5.*x+6)

>> grid on

>>hold on

>> s=x+10;

>> plot(x,s,'g');grid on

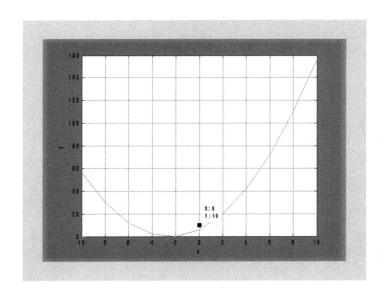

Alternatively,

>> ezplot(x.^2+5.*x+6,[-10 10])

>> grid on

>>hold on

>> s=x+10;

>> plot(x,s,'g');grid on

Draw the graph of

$$r = \frac{v^2}{i}, \, for \, i = 5$$

>> v=-10:2:10;

>> i=5;

>> r=v.^2/i;

>> plot(v,r,'g');grid on

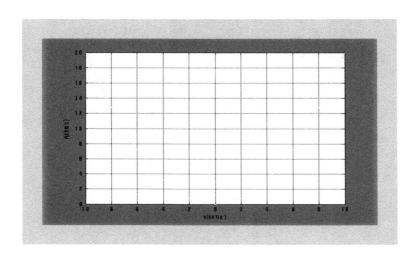

64

```
>> v=-10:2:10;

>> i=5;

>> r=v.^2/i;

>> plot(v,1./r,'r');grid on

>> subplot(2,1,1)

>> plot(v,r,'g');grid on

>> subplot(2,1,2)
```

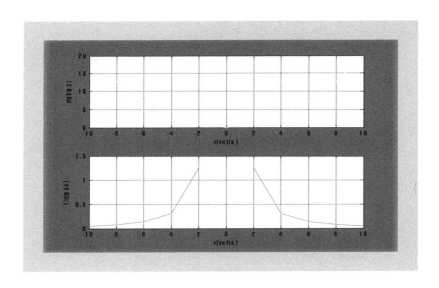

A method of solving simple equation and quadratic equation

>> solve 'x-4=10'

ans =

14

>> solve('x^2+4*x+3=0')

ans =

 -1

 -3

>> solve 'a*a'

ans =

0

0

>> solve 'x*x'

ans =

0

0

>> solve 'x^2+5*x+6'

ans =

-2

-3

```
>> solve '(x^2+4*x+3=0)'


ans =


-3
-1


>> solve '(x^3+3*x^2+3*x+1=0)'


ans =


-1
-1
-1


>> solve x^4+4*x^3+6*x^2+4*x+1
```

ans =

-1

-1

-1

-1

>> solve x^4+4*x^3+6*x^2+4*x+1=0

ans =

-1

-1

-1

-1

>> solve 'x^4+4*x^3+6*x^2+4*x+1=0'

ans =

-1

-1

-1

-1

General form of solving quadratic equation as applied in preceding task

>> solve ('a*x^2+b*x+c=0')

ans =

 -1/2*(b-(b^2-4*a*c)^(1/2))/a

 -1/2*(b+(b^2-4*a*c)^(1/2))/a

A method of solving simultaneous equation

$x + y = 2$............1

$3x - y = 10$.........2

soln

x=-10:1:10;

>> y=2-x;

>> plot(x,y,'r');grid on

>> hold on

>> y=(3*x)-10;

>> plot(x,y,'g');grid on

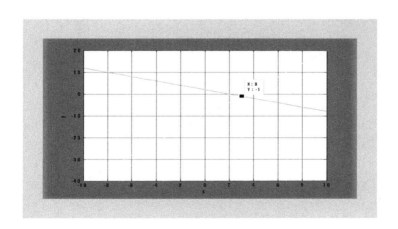

$3x - y = 10$..................1

$2x + y = 6$...................2

>> x=-10:1:10;

>> y=(3*x)-10;

>> plot(x,y,'g');grid on

>> hold on

>> y=6-(2*x);

>> plot(x,y,'m');grid on

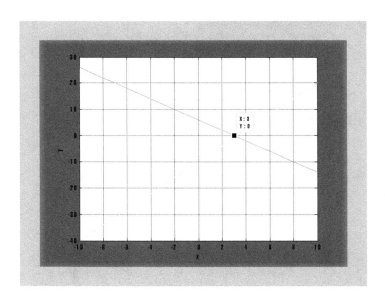

>> x=-10:1:10;

>> y=10-x;

>> plot(x,y,'r');grid on

>> hold on

72

>> y=3.*x+2;

>> plot(x,y,'m');grid on

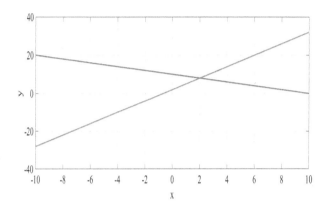

Editing the graph

Click on *Edit*. The screen is as shown below.

Scroll down to *figure properties* and click on it

Adjust the parameters to suit your requirements.

Then scroll to *copy figure* and click to copy the diagram.

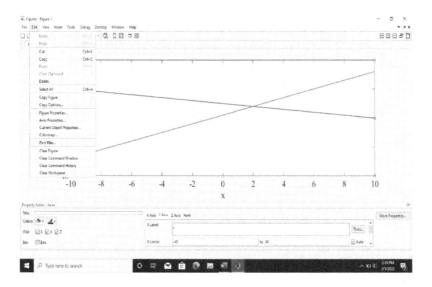

Solving two equations simultaneously

$$x + y = 3 \qquad (1)$$

$$2x - y = 5 \qquad (2)$$

Solution

>> x=-2:1:10;

>> y=3-x;

>> plot(x,y,'r');grid on

>> hold on

>> y=2.*x-5;

>> plot(x,y,'m');grid on

\>>

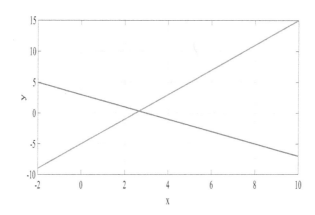

\>> syms x

\>> solve(x^2+4*x+4)

ans =

 -2

 -2

```
>> syms x
>> solve(x^2+5*x+6)

ans =

 -3

 -2

>> solve(x^2+5*x+6)

ans =

 -3

 -2
```

Use of matrix to check the graphical solution for the above question

```
>> a=[3 -1;2 1]

a =

    3  -1

    2   1

>> b=[10;6]

b =

   10

    6


>> inv(a)*b

ans =

   3.2000

  -0.4000
```

Further characteristic curves of transmission line parameters

```
>> del=0:pi/18:2*pi;

>> E=415,V=380,X=10;


E =


   415

V =


   380


>> P=V*E*sin(del)./X;

>> plot(del,P)

>> grid on

>>
```

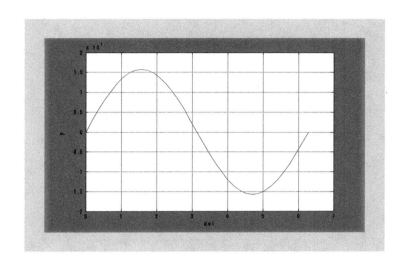

```
>> del=0:pi/18:2*pi;

>> E=415,V=380,X=10;

E =

   415

V =

   380

>> Q=(V*E*cos(del)./X)-V.^2/X;

>> plot(del,Q)

>> grid on
```

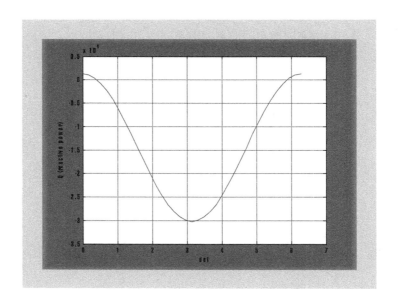

Plot of sin(x) against y where the values of x are given in radians. The use of the sign(;) to surpress the result of preceding task is as well displayed.

>> x=-pi:pi/18:pi;

>> y=sin(x)

y =

  Columns 1 through 6

  -0.0000 -0.1736 -0.3420 -0.5000 -0.6428 -0.7660

Columns 7 through 12

-0.8660 -0.9397 -0.9848 -1.0000 -0.9848 -0.9397

Columns 13 through 18

-0.8660 -0.7660 -0.6428 -0.5000 -0.3420 -0.1736

Columns 19 through 24

0 0.1736 0.3420 0.5000 0.6428 0.7660

Columns 25 through 30

0.8660 0.9397 0.9848 1.0000 0.9848 0.9397

Columns 31 through 36

0.8660 0.7660 0.6428 0.5000 0.3420 0.1736

Column 37

    0.0000

>> plot(x,y)

>> grid on

>>

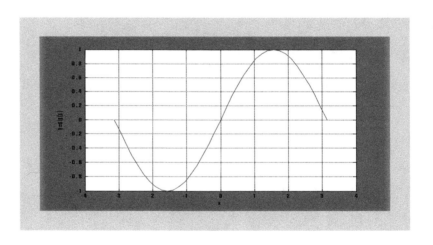

CHAPTER 5

5.0 PLOT OF VARIOUS PARAMETERS OF ELECTRIC MOTOR

```
>> x=-pi:pi/18:pi;

>> v=220*sin(x);

>> Pout=3750;

>> Pin=1.732*v*10*0.8;

>> eff=Pout./Pin;

>> plot(x,eff)

x=-pi:pi/18:pi;

>> v=220*sin(x);

>> Pout=3750;

>> Pin=1.732*v*10*0.8;

>> eff=Pout./Pin;

>> plot(x,eff)
```

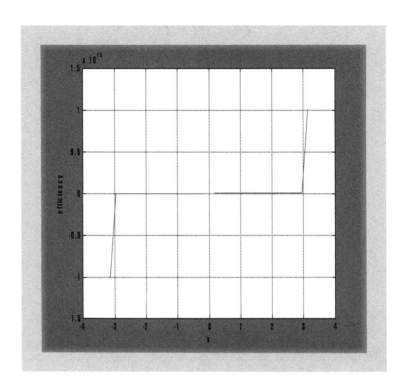

```
>>x=-pi:pi/18:pi;

>> v=220*sin(x);

>> Pout=3750;

>> Pin=1.732*v*10*0.8;

>> eff=Pout./Pin;

>> plot(v,eff)
```

>> grid on

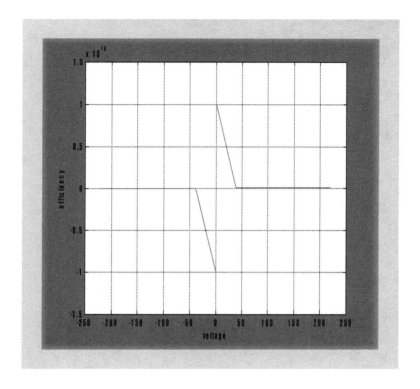

Further method of solving quadratic equations by declaring the symbols used

>> syms x y

>> x.^2+4*x+4

ans =

x^2+4*x+4

```
>> factor(ans)

ans =

(x+2)^2

>> syms x y

>> y=x.^3+45*x.^2+4100*x+14500

y =

x^3+45*x^2+4100*x+14500

>> factor(y)

 ans =

x^3+45*x^2+4100*x+14500

>> factor(ans)

ans =

x^3+45*x^2+4100*x+14500

 >> syms x y

>> x.^3+45*x.^2+4100*x+14500

 ans =

x^3+45*x^2+4100*x+14500
```

>> factor(ans)

ans =

x^3+45*x^2+4100*x+14500

>> expand(ans)

ans =

x^3+45*x^2+4100*x+14500

>> syms x

>> x.^3+45*x.^2+4100*x+14500

ans =

x^3+45*x^2+4100*x+14500

>> factor(ans)

ans =

x^3+45*x^2+4100*x+14500

>> solve('x^2+y^2=9')

ans =

(-y^2+9)^(1/2)

-(-y^2+9)^(1/2)

Alternatively,

>> syms x y

>> solve('x^2+y^2=9')

ans =

  (-y^2+9)^(1/2)

  -(-y^2+9)^(1/2)

 Solution to quadratic equation and a method of plotting the graph

>> solve('x^2+4*x+4=0')

 ans =

 -2

 -2

>> ezplot('x^2+4*x+4',[-10 10])

>> grid on

>> ezplot('sin(x)',[-pi pi])

>> hold on

>> ezplot('10-x',[0 10])

>> grid on

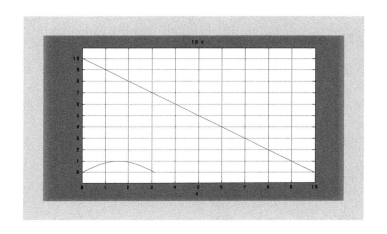

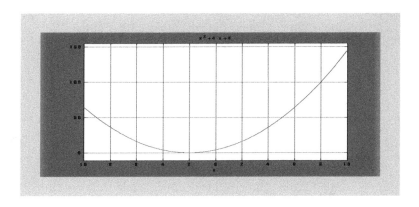

Solving equations that involve three variables

>> syms x y z

>> solve{'3*x+4*y*5*z=2

??? solve{'3*x+4*y*5*z=2

Error: A MATLAB string constant is not terminated properly.

>> solve('3*x+4*y+5*z=2,2*x-3*y+7*z=-1,x-6*y+z=3')

ans =

  x: [1x1 sym]

  y: [1x1 sym]

  z: [1x1 sym]

Alternatively

>> s=[3 4 5;2 -3 7;1 -6 1]

s =

   3   4   5

   2   -3   7

   1   -6   1

>> t=[2;-1;3]

t =

   2

  -1

3

```
>> u=inv(s)*t

u =

    2.6196

   -0.2283

   -0.9891

>> syms x y

>> x^4-y^4

ans =

 x^4-y^4

>> factor(ans)

ans =

(x-y)*(x+y)*(x^2+y^2)

>> sym x

ans =

x

>> solve('x^2+y^2+10*x+10*y+25=0')
```

ans =

-5+(-y^2-10*y)^(1/2)

-5-(-y^2-10*y)^(1/2)

> solve('x^2+y^2+10*x+10*y+25=0')

ans =

-5+(-y^2-10*y)^(1/2)

-5-(-y^2-10*y)^(1/2)

>> simplify

??? Input argument "a" is undefined.

Error in ==> simplify at 24

out = a;

>> simplify(ans)

ans =

-5+(-y*(y+10))^(1/2)

-5-(-y*(y+10))^(1/2)

Plot of graph that involve three variables

```
teta=-pi:pi/18:pi;beta=3*pi/2;
r=10;
x=r.*sin(teta)*cos(beta);
y=r.*sin(teta)*sin(beta);
z=r*cos(teta);
plot(teta,x,'r');grid on
subplot(2,2,1);
plot(teta,y,'m');grid on
subplot(2,2,2);
plot(teta,z,'c');grid on
subplot(2,2,3);
plot(teta,x,y,z,'g');grid on
subplot(2,2,4);
```

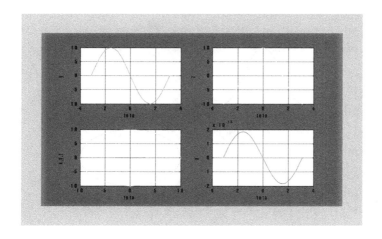

```
teta=-pi/2:pi/18:pi/2;beta=3*pi/2;
r=10;
x=r.*sin(teta)*cos(beta);
y=r.*sin(teta)*sin(beta);
z=r*cos(teta);
plot(teta,x,'r');grid on
subplot(2,2,1);
plot(teta,y,'m');grid on
subplot(2,2,2);
plot(teta,z,'c');grid on
subplot(2,2,3);
plot(teta,x,y,z,'g');grid on
subplot(2,2,4);
```

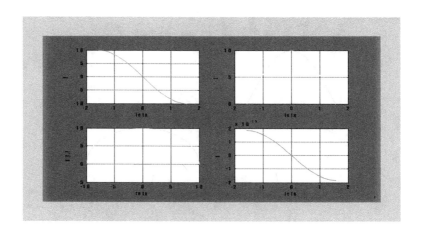

```
teta=-2*pi:pi/18:2*pi;beta=3*pi/2;
r=10;
x=r.*sin(teta)*cos(beta);
y=r.*sin(teta)*sin(beta);
z=r*cos(teta);
plot(teta,x,'r');grid on
subplot(2,2,1);
plot(teta,y,'m');grid on
subplot(2,2,2);
plot(teta,z,'c');grid on
subplot(2,2,3);
plot(teta,x,y,z,'g');grid on
subplot(2,2,4);
```

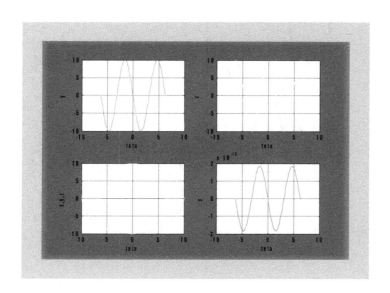

```
teta=-2*pi:pi/18:2*pi;beta=3*pi/2;
r=10;
x=r.*sin(teta)*cos(beta);
y=r.*sin(teta)*sin(beta);
z=r*sin(teta);
plot(teta,x,'r');grid on
subplot(2,2,1);
plot(teta,y,'m');grid on
subplot(2,2,2);
plot(teta,z,'c');grid on
subplot(2,2,3);
plot(teta,x,y,z,'g');grid on
subplot(2,2,4);
```

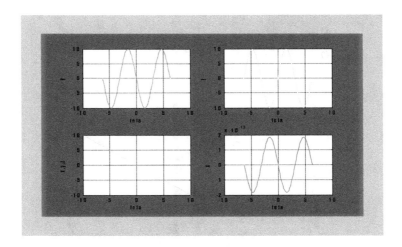

CHAPTER 6

6.0 SOLVING DIFFERENTIAL EQUATIONS

>> syms x

>> diff(x^4)*{remember no gap in between diff and (x^4)}*

 ans =

 4*x^3

>> syms x y

>> dsolve('D2y-2*Dy-3*y=0')

ans =

C1*exp(3*t)+C2*exp(-t)

>> syms x y

>> dsolve('Dy=-y-3*x,y(0)=1')

ans =

-3*x+exp(-t)*(1+3*x)

>> syms x y

>> dsolve('Dy=-y-3*x')

ans =

-3*x+exp(-t)*C1

A method of solving third order equation
>> syms x

>> solve ('x^3+45*x^2+4100*x+14500')
*{remember there is gap in between solve and ('x^3+45*x^2+4100*x+14500')}*

ans =

  5/3*(4347+6*2453415^(1/2))^(1/3)-
685/(4347+6*2453415^(1/2))^(1/3)-15

  -
5/6*(4347+6*2453415^(1/2))^(1/3)+685/2/(4347+
6*2453415^(1/2))^(1/3)-
15+5/2*i*3^(1/2)*(1/3*(4347+6*2453415^(1/2))^
(1/3)+137/(4347+6*2453415^(1/2))^(1/3))

-
5/6*(4347+6*2453415^(1/2))^(1/3)+685/2/(4347+
6*2453415^(1/2))^(1/3)-15-
5/2*i*3^(1/2)*(1/3*(4347+6*2453415^(1/2))^(1/3
)+137/(4347+6*2453415^(1/2))^(1/3))

>> simplify(ans)

ans =

5/3*((4347+6*2453415^(1/2))^(2/3)-411-
9*(4347+6*2453415^(1/2))^(1/3))/(4347+6*24534
15^(1/2))^(1/3)

5/6*(-(4347+6*3^(1/2)*817805^(1/2))^(2/3)+411-
18*(4347+6*3^(1/2)*817805^(1/2))^(1/3)+i*3^(1/
2)*(4347+6*3^(1/2)*817805^(1/2))^(2/3)+411*i*
3^(1/2))/(4347+6*3^(1/2)*817805^(1/2))^(1/3)

-5/6*((4347+6*3^(1/2)*817805^(1/2))^(2/3)-
411+18*(4347+6*3^(1/2)*817805^(1/2))^(1/3)+i*
3^(1/2)*(4347+6*3^(1/2)*817805^(1/2))^(2/3)+41
1*i*3^(1/2))/(4347+6*3^(1/2)*817805^(1/2))^(1/3
)

Solving quadratic equation

```
>> syms x

>> solve ('x^2+20*x+2900')

ans =


-10+20*i*7^(1/2)

-10-20*i*7^(1/2)
```

Solving quadratic equation and showing the graph of the result

```
>> syms x

>> solve ('x^2+20*x+2900')

ans =

-10+20*i*7^(1/2)

-10-20*i*7^(1/2)

>> ezplot(x.^2+20*x+2900,[2 10])
```

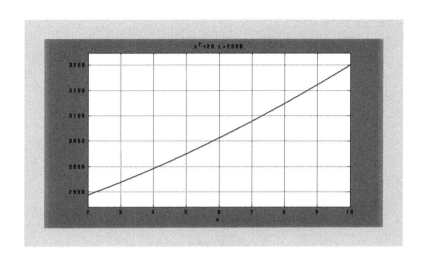

>> ezplot(cos(x),[-pi pi])

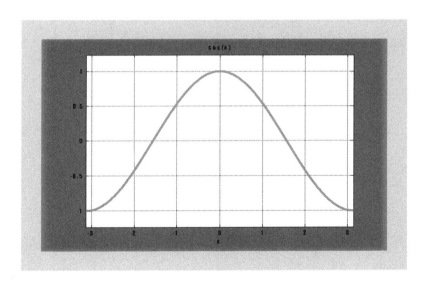

\>\> ezplot(sin(x)),[-pi,pi]

ans =

-3.1416   3.1416

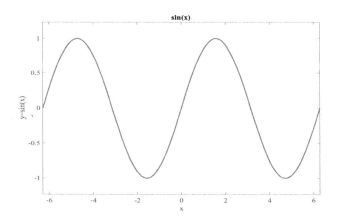

>> ezplot(sin(x))

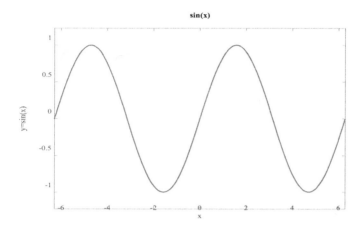

>> syms teta

>> ezplot(sin(teta))

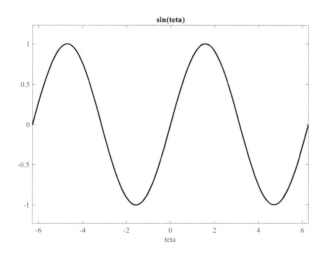

>> ezplot(cos(x)),[-2*pi 2*pi]

ans =

   -6.2832   6.2832

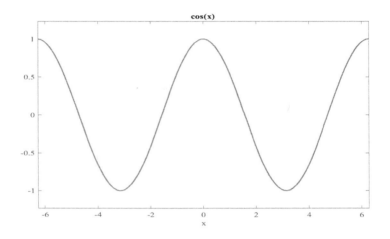

>> ezplot(tan(x)),[-pi pi]

ans =

   -3.1416   3.1416

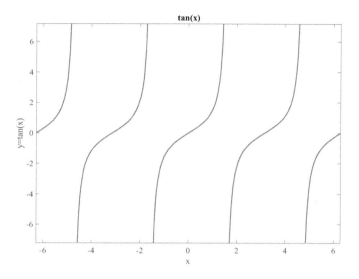

>> syms teta

>> ezplot(sec(teta))

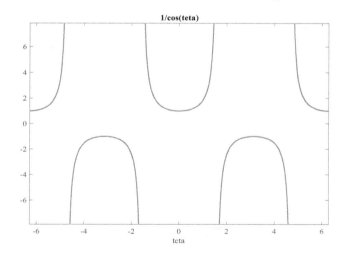

```
>> syms s

>> solve (s^2+5*s+6)

ans =

 -2

 -3

 >> ezplot(s.^2+5*s+6,[-10 10])

>> grid on
```

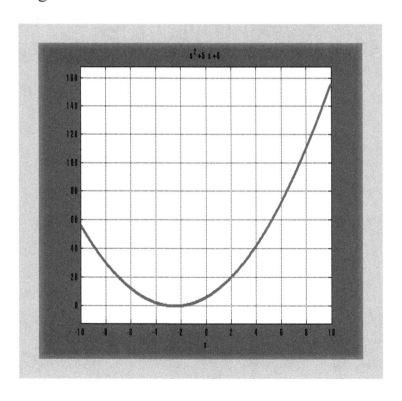

>> ezplot(s.^2+5.*s+6)

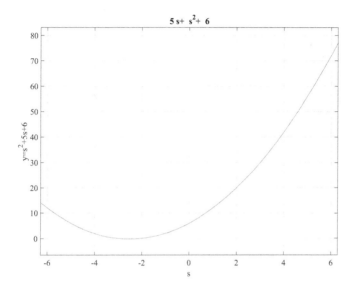

Method of presenting two results on a graph

>> ezplot(s.^2+5*s+6,[-10 10])

>> grid on

>>//// hold on

>> ezplot(10-s,[-10 10])

>>

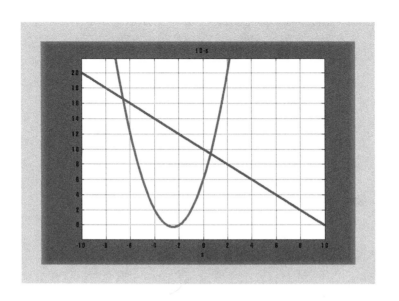

Application of (') in solving problems

>> syms x y z

>>solve(10*x+3*y+z=10,5*x+6*y+4*z=0,3*x+6*y+5*z=0)

???
solve(10*x+3*y+z=10,5*x+6*y+4*z=0,3*x+6*y+5*z=0)

Error: The expression to the left of the equals sign is not a

valid target for an assignment.

solve('10*x+3*y+z=10,5*x+6*y+4*z=0,3*x+6*y+5*z=0')

ans =

  x: [1x1 sym]

  y: [1x1 sym]

  z: [1x1 sym]

\>> simplify(ans)

ans =

  x: [1x1 sym]

  y: [1x1 sym]

  z: [1x1 sym]

Alternatively

\>> a=[10 3 1;5 6 4;3 6 5]

a =

  10   3   1

   5   6   4

   3   6   5

\>> b=[10;0;0]

b =

   10

    0

    0

\>> c=inv(a)*b

c =

   1.8182

  -3.9394

   3.6364

That is

x=1.8182, y=-3.9394 & z=3.6364

CHAPTER 7

7.0 METHOD OF SOLVING MATRIX WITH INDICATION OF PROBABLE ERROR

\>> a=[10 3 1,5 6 4,3 6 5];

\>> b=[10,0,0];

\>> inv(a)

??? Error using ==> inv

Matrix must be square.

\>> a=[10 3 1,5 6 4,3 6 5]

a =

    10   3   1   5   6   4   3   6   5

\>> a=[10 3 1;5 6 4;3 6 5;]

a =

```
    10   3   1

     5   6   4

     3   6   5
>> a=ones(3)


a =


     1   1   1

     1   1   1

     1   1   1


>> b=[10;0;0]


b =


    10

     0
```

0

>> inv(a)

ans =

```
    0.1818   -0.2727    0.1818
   -0.3939    1.4242   -1.0606
    0.3636   -1.5455    1.3636
```

>> inv(a)*b

ans =

```
    1.8182
   -3.9394
    3.6364
```

Solving $\quad x + 2y + 4z = 3,$

$2x + 2y + 3z = 4$

$3x + 4y + 5z = 5$

using matrix

$$a * c = f$$

$$c = a^{-1} \times f$$

\>> a=[1 2 4;2 2 3;3 4 5];

\>> f=[3;4;5];

\>> c=inv(a)*f

c =

2.0000

-1.5000

1.0000

\>> a=[1 2 4;2 2 3;3 4 5];

\>> f=[3;4;5];

>> c=inv(a)*f

c =

  2.0000

  -1.5000

  1.0000

>> det(a)

ans =

  4

Solving $x_1 + 2x_2 - 12x_3 + 8x_4 = 27$

$5x_1 + 4x_2 + 7x_3 - 2x_4 = 4$

$-3x_1 + 7x_2 + 9x_3 + 5x_4 = 11$

$6x_1 - 12x_2 - 8x_3 + 3x_4 = 49$

Using matrix

>> A=[1 2 -12 8;5 4 7 -2;-3 7 9 5;6 -12 -8 3];

>> B=[27;4;11;49];

>> x=inv(A)*B

x =

  3.0000

-2.0000

  1.0000

  5.0000

i.e $x_1 = 3, x_2 =- 2, x_3 = 1, x_4 = 5$

Plot of graph involving two variables
>> syms x y

>> illum=300/(4*pi*((x-5)^2+(y-2)^2+9))

illum =75/pi/((x-5)^2+(y-2)^2+9)

>> ezcontourf(illum,[0 10 0 4])

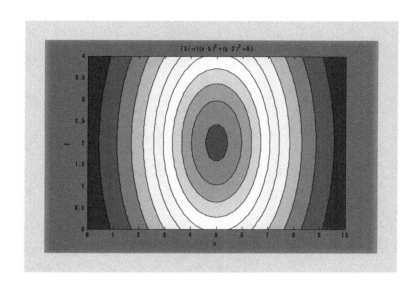

Plot of graph involving two variables with a specified color (gray)

>> ezcontourf(illum,[0 10 0 4]);colormap(gray);axis equal tight

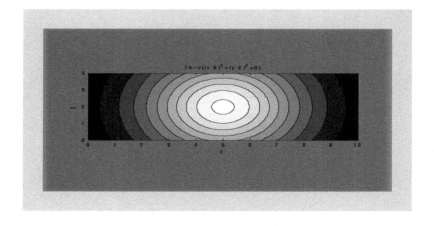

??? Undefined function or variable 'red'.

>> ezplot(x.^3,[-10 10]);colormap(gray)

>> ezplot(x.^3,[-10 10]);colormap(black)

??? Undefined function or variable 'black'.

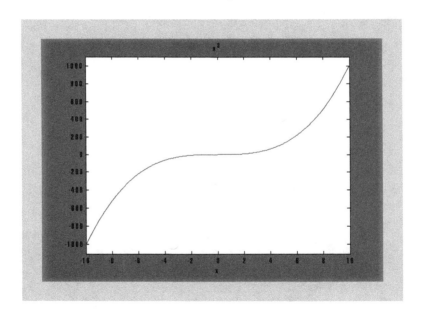

CHAPTER 8

8.0 PLOT OF VOLTAGE VARIATION AGAINST EFFICIENCY OF ELECTRIC MOTOR TAKEN A RANDOM VALUE FOR THE CURRENT CONSUMPTION

v= [300:20:420];

>> Pout=3750;

>> i=8;

>> Pin=1.732*v*i*0.8;

>> eff=Pout./Pin

eff =

    1.1277   1.0572   0.9950   0.9397   0.8903
0.8458   0.8055

>> plot(v,eff) >>

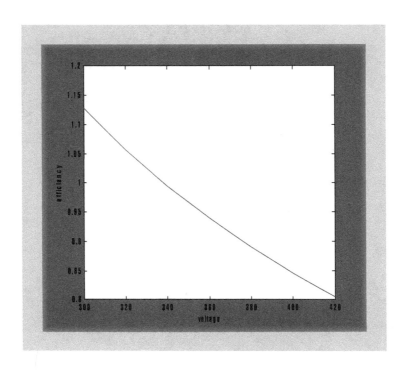

Further plot of parameters with indication of common mistakes

freq=[0:10:50];

>> p=2;

>> N=120*f./p;

??? Undefined function or variable 'f'.

>> N=120*freq./p;

```
>> t=10;

>> v=415*sin(2*3.142*f*t);

??? Undefined function or variable 'f'.

>> v=415*sin(2*3.142*freq*t);

>> plot(freq,v)

>> freq=[0:10:50];

>> p=2;

>> N=120*f./p;

??? Undefined function or variable 'f'.

>> N=120*freq./p;

>> t=10;

>> v=415*sin(2*3.142*f*t);

??? Undefined function or variable 'f'.

>> v=415*sin(2*3.142*freq*t);

>> plot(freq,v)

>>>> freq=[0:10:50];

>> p=2;

>> N=120*f./p;
```

??? Undefined function or variable 'f'.

```
>> N=120*freq./p;

>> t=10;

>> v=415*sin(2*3.142*f*t);
```

??? Undefined function or variable 'f'.

```
>> v=415*sin(2*3.142*freq*t);

>> plot(freq,v)

>> freq=[0:10:50];

>> p=2;

>> N=120*f./p;
```

??? Undefined function or variable 'f'.

```
>> N=120*freq./p;

>> t=10;

>> v=415*sin(2*3.142*f*t);
```

??? Undefined function or variable 'f'.

```
>> v=415*sin(2*3.142*freq*t);

>> plot(freq,v)
```

>>

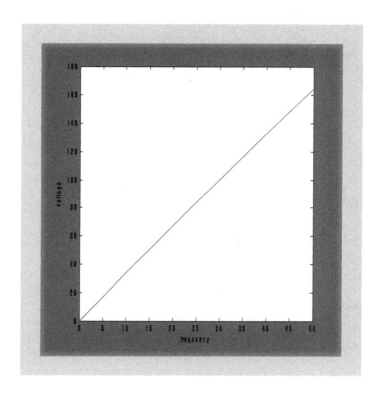

>> freq=[0:10:50];

>> p=2;

>> N=120*freq./p;

>> t=60;

>> v=415*sin(2*3.142*freq*t);

>> plot(freq,v)

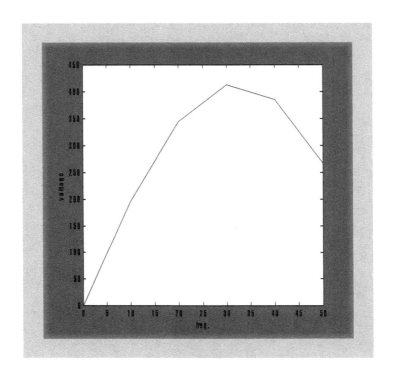

```
>> freq=[0:10:50];

>> p=2;

>> N=120*freq./p;

>> t=120;

>> v=415*sin(2*3.142*freq*t);

>> plot(freq,v)
```

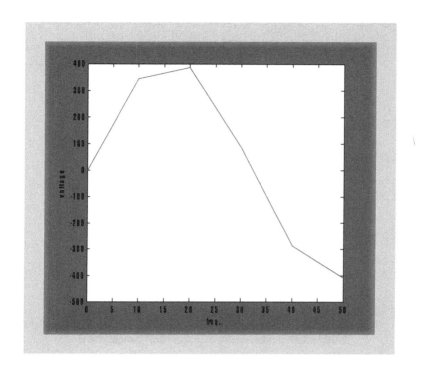

>> v=[0:50:420];

>> Pout=3750;

>> i=8;

>> eff=Pout./(1.732*v*i*0.8)

eff =

  Columns 1 through 6

Inf   6.7660   3.3830   2.2553   1.6915
1.3532

Columns 7 through 9

1.1277   0.9666   0.8458

>> plot(v,eff)

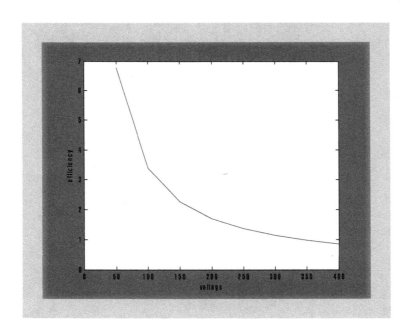

```
> t=0:2:10;
>> y=2*exp(-3*t)-exp(-2*t);
>> plot(t,y,'r');grid on
```

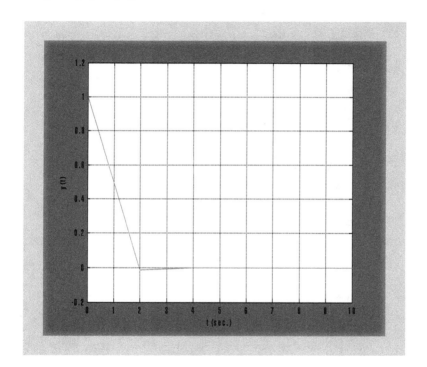

```
>> t=0:0.01:1;
>> y=2*exp(-3*t)-exp(-2*t);
>> plot(t,y,'b');grid on
```

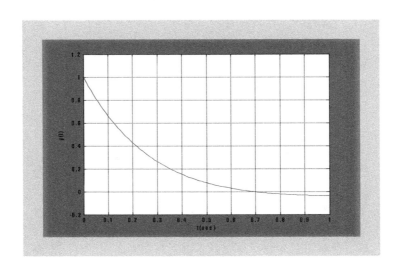

>> t=0:0.1:1;

>> f=exp(t);

>> plot(t,y,'r');grid on

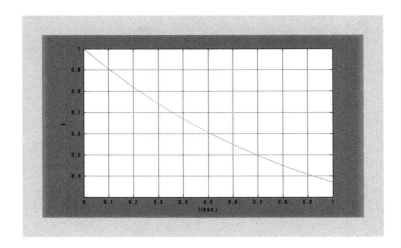

```
>> t=0:0.1:1;

>> q=exp(-t);

>> plot(t,q,'m');grid on
```

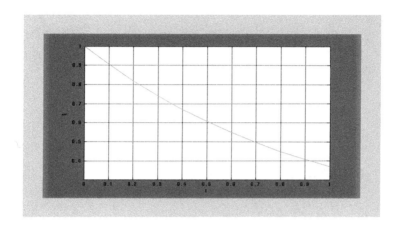

```
>> t=0:0.1:1;

>> m=1-exp(-t);

>> plot(t,m,'g');grid on
```

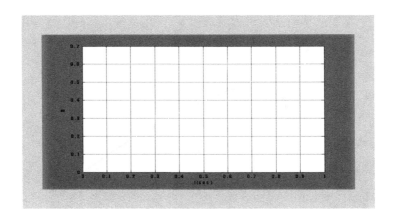

>> t=0:0.1:1;

>> n=1-exp(t);

>> plot(t,n,'c');grid on

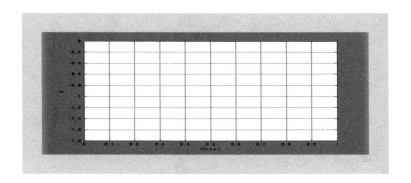

CHAPTER 9

9.0 PLOT OF ELECTRIC MOTOR FREQUENCY AND TORQUE

```
>> freq=[0:10:50];

>> P=3750;

>> p=2;

>> T=P*p./(240*pi*freq)


T =


    Inf    0.9947    0.4974    0.3316    0.2487
0.1989


>> plot(freq,T)

>>
```

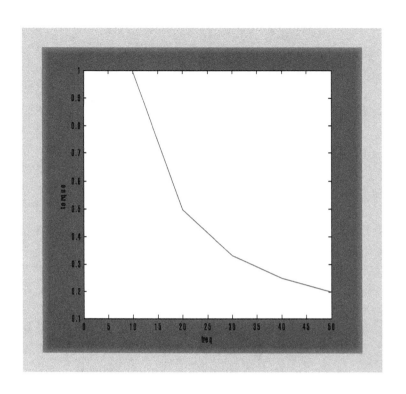

>> freq=[0:5:50]

freq =

  Columns 1 through 10

   0   5   10   15   20   25   30   35   40   45

  Column 11

   50

\>> P=3750;

\>> p=4;

\>> T=P*p./(240*3.142*freq)

T =

 Columns 1 through 6

    Inf   3.9784   1.9892   1.3261   0.9946
0.7957

 Columns 7 through 11

    0.6631   0.5683   0.4973   0.4420   0.3978

\>> plot(freq,T);

\>> grid on

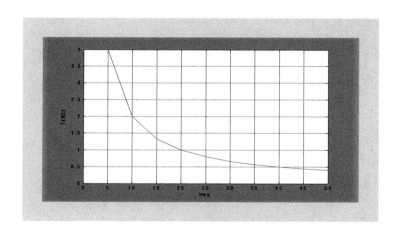

```
v=[300:10:420];
i=10;
Pout=3750;
eff=Pout./(1.732*v*i*0.8);
plot(v,eff)
grid on
```

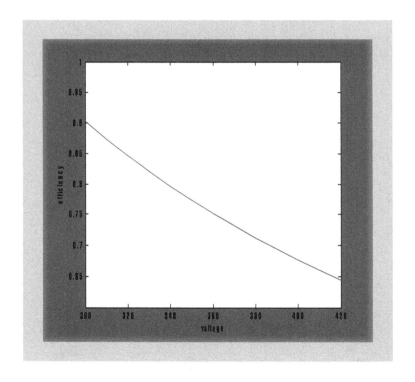

>> v=0:20:415;

>> Pout=3750;

>> Pin=1.732*v*10*0.8;

```
>> eff=Pout./Pin

eff =

  Columns 1 through 6


    Inf  13.5320   6.7660   4.5107   3.3830
2.7064

  Columns 7 through 12

   2.2553   1.9331   1.6915   1.5036   1.3532
1.2302

  Columns 13 through 18

   1.1277   1.0409   0.9666   0.9021   0.8458
0.7960

  Columns 19 through 21

   0.7518   0.7122   0.6766

>> plot(v,eff)

>> grid on
```

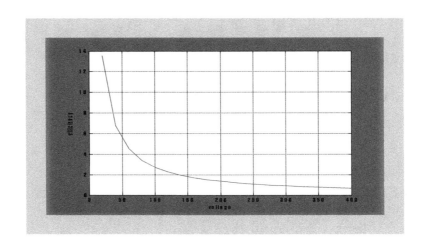

CHAPTER 10

10.0 DETERMINATION OF AC MOTOR EFFICIENCY

```
>> v=0:20:415;

>> Pout=7500;

>> Pin=1.732*v*10*0.8;

>> eff=Pout./Pin

eff =

  Columns 1 through 6

    Inf   27.0641   13.5320   9.0214   6.7660
5.4128
```

Columns 7 through 12

　4.5107　3.8663　3.3830　3.0071　2.7064
2.4604

Columns 13 through 18

　2.2553　2.0819　1.9331　1.8043　1.6915
1.5920

Columns 19 through 21

   1.5036   1.4244   1.3532

\>> plot(v,eff)

\>> grid on

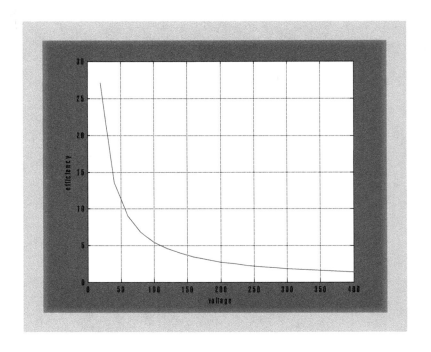

\>> v=0:20:415;

\>> Pout=15000;

\>> Pin=1.732*v*10*0.8;

\>> eff=Pout./Pin;

```
>> plot(v,eff)

>> grid on
```

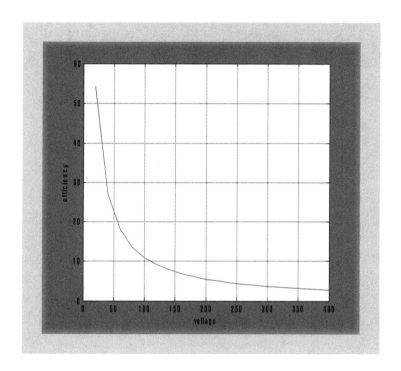

```
function pi = fcn(v,r,l,i)
% This block supports the Embedded MATLAB
subset.
% See the help menu for details.

pi = (v-r*i)/l;

>> teta=0:pi/18:pi/2;
>> w=7500;
>> pf=cos(teta);
```

```
>> va=w./pf;
>> plot(pf,va)
>> grid on
```

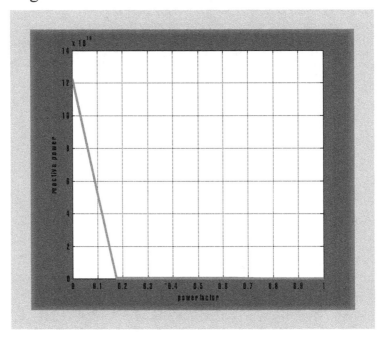

```
>> teta=0:pi/18:pi/2;

>> va=5000;

>> pf=cos(teta);

>> w=va*pf;

>> plot(pf,w)

>> grid on
```

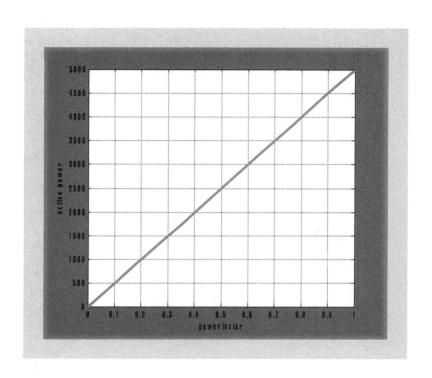

```
>> teta=0:pi/18:2*pi;

>> w=1000;

>> va=w./cos(teta);

>> plot(teta,va)

>> grid on
```

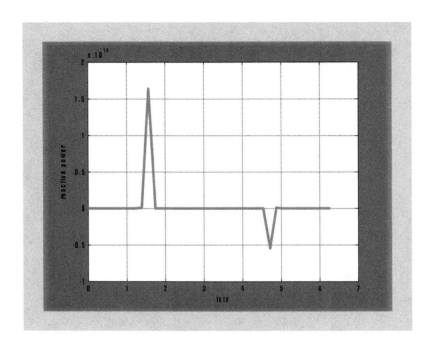

```
>> teta=0:pi/18:2*pi;

>> w=1000;

>> va=w./cos(teta);

>> var=w./cos(teta);

>> va=sqrt(w.^2+va.^2);

>> plot(teta,va)

>> grid on
```

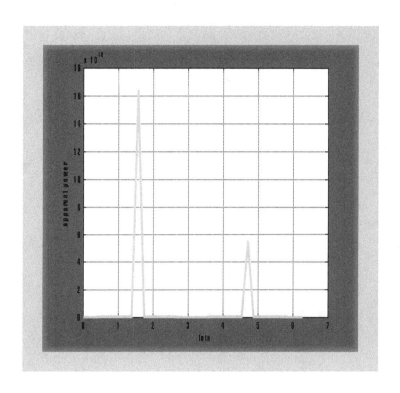

```
>> teta=0:pi/18:2*pi;

>> pf=cos(teta);

>> w=1000;

>> var=w./cos(teta);

>> va=sqrt(w.^2+var.^2);

>> plot(pf,va)

>> grid on
```

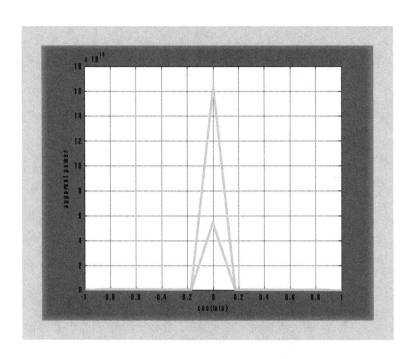

```
>> teta=0:pi/18:2*pi;

>> pf=cos(teta);

>> w=1000;

>> var=w./cos(teta);

>> plot(pf,var)

>> grid on
```

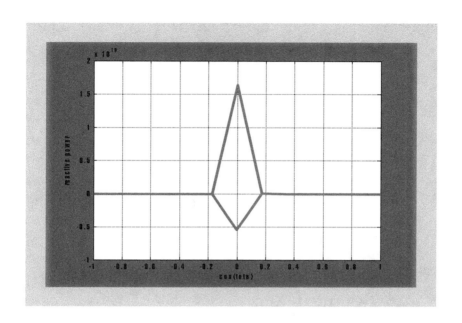

CHAPTER 11

11.0 The use of m-file has some advantages over the command window. One of the advantages is that error could be corrected when using m-file after entering some commands.

```
Lm=0.035;rs=0.3;rr=15;Lls=0.0015;Llr=0.0007;p=
2;w=377;s=0:0.1:1;
we=(2./p)*w;Xm=w*Lm;Xls=w*Lls;Xlr=w*Llr;V
as=208/3^0.5;
Za=Xm*(Xlr+rr./s);
Zb=(Xlr+rr./s)+Xm;
Zr=Za./Zb;
Zs=rs+Xls+Zr;
Ias=Vas./Zs;
Iar=(Ias*Xm)./(Xlr+rr./s+Xm);
Pm=3.*Iar.^2.*rr.*(1-s)./s;
T=(3.*Pm.*Iar.^2.*rr)./2.*w.*s;
wr=(1-s)*we;
N=(60*wr)/2*pi;
plot(s,T)
grid on
plot(s,Iar)
grid on
plot(Pm,T)
grid on
plot(Iar,T)
grid on
plot(s,N)
```

grid on

As shown in the following figure such command will only respond to the last task, that is plot of (s,N). The method to draw all the graphs on a page will be discussed later.

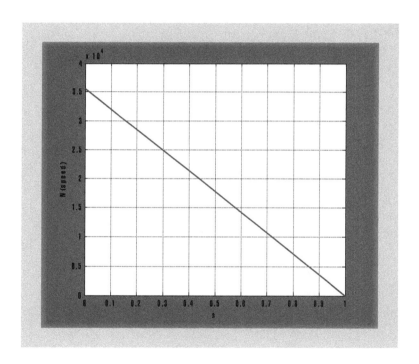

11.1 DETERMINATION OF ELECTRICAL MACHINE PARAMETERS

>> s=0:0.1:1;

>>Lm=0.035;rs=0.3;rt=15;LIs=0.0015;LIr=0.0007;P=2;w=377;

>> we=(2./P)*w;

>> Xm=w*Lm;

>> XIs=w*LIs;

>> XIr=w*LIr;

>> Vas=208/(3^0.5);

>> Za=Xm*(XIr+rt./s);

>> Zb=(XIr+rt./s)+Xm;

>> Zr=Za./Zb;

>> Zs=rs+XIs+Zr;

>> Ias=Vas./Zs;

>> Iar=(Ias*Xm)./(XIr+rt./s+Xm);

>> Pm=3.*Iar.^2.*rt.*(1-s)./s;

>> T=(3.*Pm.*Iar.^2.*rt)./(2.*w.*s);

```
>> wr=(1-s)*we;

>> N=(60*wr)/(2*pi);

>> plot(s,T);grid on
```

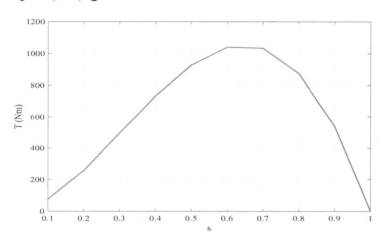

```
>> s=0:0.1:1;

>>Lm=0.035;rs=0.3;rt=15;LIs=0.0015;LIr=0.0007
;P=2;w=377;

>> we=(2./P)*w;

>> Xm=w*Lm;

>> XIs=w*LIs;

>> XIr=w*LIr;

>> Vas=208/(3^0.5);

>> Za=Xm*(XIr+rt./s);
```

```
>> Zb=(XIr+rt./s)+Xm;

>> Zr=Za./Zb;

>> Zs=rs+XIs+Zr;

>> Ias=Vas./Zs;

>> Iar=(Ias*Xm)./(XIr+rt./s+Xm);

>> Pm=3.*Iar.^2.*rt.*(1-s)./s;

>> T=(3.*Pm.*Iar.^2.*rt)./(2.*w.*s);

>> wr=(1-s)*we;

>> N=(60*wr)/(2*pi);

>> plot(s,Pm);grid on
```

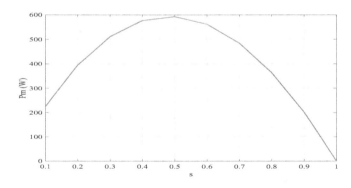

```
>> s=0:0.1:1;
>>Lm=0.035;rs=0.3;rt=15;LIs=0.0015;LIr=0.0007
;P=2;w=377;
>> we=(2./P)*w;
>> Xm=w*Lm;
>> XIs=w*LIs;
>> XIr=w*LIr;
>> Vas=208/(3^0.5);
>> Za=Xm*(XIr+rt./s);
>> Zb=(XIr+rt./s)+Xm;
>> Zr=Za./Zb;
>> Zs=rs+XIs+Zr;
>> Ias=Vas./Zs;
>> Iar=(Ias*Xm)./(XIr+rt./s+Xm);
>> Pm=3.*Iar.^2.*rt.*(1-s)./s;
>> T=(3.*Pm.*Iar.^2.*rt)./(2.*w.*s);
>> wr=(1-s)*we;
>> N=(60*wr)/(2*pi);
>> plot(T,Pm);grid on
```

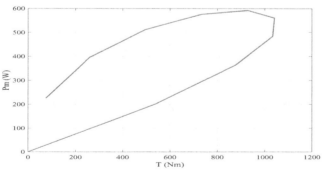

```
>> s=0:0.1:1;
>>Lm=0.035;rs=0.3;rt=15;LIs=0.0015;LIr=0.0007
;P=2;w=377;
>> we=(2./P)*w;
>> Xm=w*Lm;
>> XIs=w*LIs;
>> XIr=w*LIr;
>> Vas=208/(3^0.5);
>> Za=Xm*(XIr+rt./s);
>> Zb=(XIr+rt./s)+Xm;
>> Zr=Za./Zb;
>> Zs=rs+XIs+Zr;
>> Ias=Vas./Zs;
>> Iar=(Ias*Xm)./(XIr+rt./s+Xm);
>> Pm=3.*Iar.^2.*rt.*(1-s)./s;
>> T=(3.*Pm.*Iar.^2.*rt)./(2.*w.*s);
>> wr=(1-s)*we;
>> N=(60*wr)/(2*pi);
>> plot(Iar,T);grid on
```

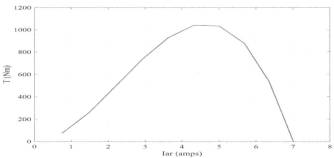

CHAPTER 11

11.0 Determination of polynomial when the roots of the polynomial are given

Example 1

Given the roots of equation as -2 twice

```
>> r=[-2 -2]
```

r =

   -2   -2

```
>> p=poly(r)
```

p =

   1   4   4

The equation, is x^2+4*x+4=0

Example 2

For the roots of an equation as 1, 2 and 1

>> r=[1 2 1]

r =

   1   2   1

>> poly(r)

ans =

   1 -4   5 -2

i.e $x^3-4x^2+5x-2=0$

Example 3

>> i=sqrt(-1)

i =

    0 + 1.0000i

>> r=[-1 -2 -3+4*i -3-4*i]

r =

Columns 1 through 3

-1.0000   -2.0000   -3.0000 + 4.0000i

Column 4

-3.0000 - 4.0000i

>> p=poly(r)

p =

    1   9   45   87   50

therefore the equation is,
x^4+9x^3+45x^2+87x+50=0

Example 4

>> a=[2 3 4];

>> p=poly(a)

p =

    1   -9   26   -24

that is a^3-9*a^2+26*a-24=0

```
>> s=[-5 -20+j*50 -20-j*50]

s =

 -5.0000          -20.0000 +50.0000i -20.0000 -
50.0000i

>> R=poly(s)

R =

         1       45      3100      14500

>> i.e R(s)=s^3+45*s^2+3100*s+14500=0

>> teta=0:pi/18:2*pi;

>> V=220*sin(teta);r=10;C=0.0001;L=0.001;

>>Ir=V./r;Ic=C.*cos(teta)*220;Il=220*cos(teta)./L
;

>>Ir=V./r;Ic=C.*cos(teta)*220;Il=220*cos(teta)./L

Il =

 1.0e+005 *

 Columns 1 through 6

  2.2000   2.1666   2.0673   1.9053   1.6853
1.4141
```

Columns 7 through 12

   1.1000   0.7524   0.3820   0.0000   -0.3820   -0.7524

Columns 13 through 18

   -1.1000   -1.4141   -1.6853   -1.9053   -2.0673   -2.1666

Columns 19 through 24

   -2.2000   -2.1666   -2.0673   -1.9053   -1.6853   -1.4141

Columns 25 through 30

   -1.1000   -0.7524   -0.3820   -0.0000   0.3820   0.7524

Columns 31 through 36

   1.1000   1.4141   1.6853   1.9053   2.0673   2.1666

Column 37

   2.2000

>> plot(teta,Ir)

>> grid on

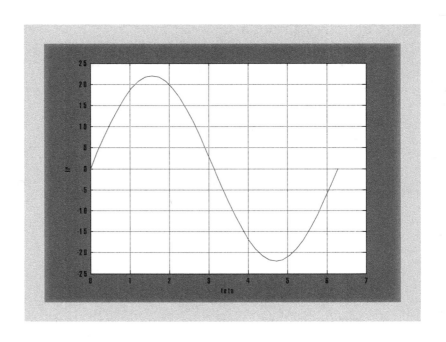

>> teta=0:pi/18:2*pi;

>> V=220*sin(teta);r=10;C=0.0001;L=0.001;

>>
Ir=V./r;Ic=C.*cos(teta)*220;Il=220*cos(teta)./L;

>>
Ir=V./r;Ic=C.*cos(teta)*220;Il=220*cos(teta)./L

Il =

  1.0e+005 *

  Columns 1 through 6

2.2000   2.1666   2.0673   1.9053   1.6853
1.4141

Columns 7 through 12

1.1000   0.7524   0.3820   0.0000   -0.3820   -
0.7524

Columns 13 through 18

-1.1000   -1.4141   -1.6853   -1.9053   -2.0673   -
2.1666

Columns 19 through 24

-2.2000   -2.1666   -2.0673   -1.9053   -1.6853   -
1.4141

Columns 25 through 30

-1.1000   -0.7524   -0.3820   -0.0000   0.3820
0.7524

Columns 31 through 36

1.1000   1.4141   1.6853   1.9053   2.0673
2.1666

Column 37

  2.2000

>> plot(teta,Ir)

>> grid on

>> plot(teta,Ic)

>> grid on

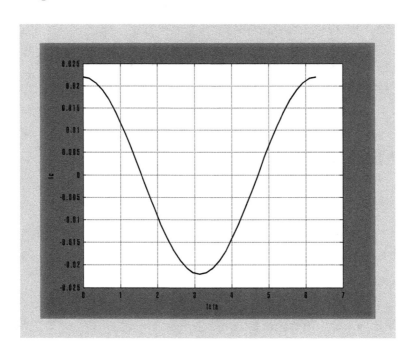

CHAPTER 12

12.0 PLOT OF PHASE ANGLE AGAINST RESPECTIVE CURRENTS IN AN RLC CIRCUIT

>> teta=0:pi/18:2*pi;

>> V=220*sin(teta);r=10;C=0.0001;L=0.001;

>>
Ir=V./r;Ic=C.*cos(teta)*220;Il=220*cos(teta)./L;

>>
Ir=V./r;Ic=C.*cos(teta)*220;Il=220*cos(teta)./L

Il =

1.0e+005 *

Columns 1 through 6

2.2000   2.1666   2.0673   1.9053   1.6853
1.4141

Columns 7 through 12

1.1000   0.7524   0.3820   0.0000   -0.3820   -0.7524

Columns 13 through 18

-1.1000   -1.4141   -1.6853   -1.9053   -2.0673   -2.1666

Columns 19 through 24

-2.2000   -2.1666   -2.0673   -1.9053   -1.6853   -1.4141

Columns 25 through 30

-1.1000   -0.7524   -0.3820   -0.0000   0.3820   0.7524

Columns 31 through 36

   1.1000   1.4141   1.6853   1.9053   2.0673
2.1666

Column 37

   2.2000

>> plot(teta,Ir)

>> grid on

>> plot(teta,Ic)

>> grid on

>> plot(teta,Il)

>> grid on

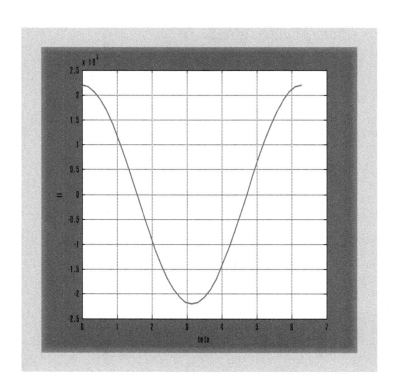

>> teta=0:pi/18:2*pi;

>> V=220*sin(teta);r=10;C=0.0001;L=0.001;

>>
Ir=V./r;Ic=C.*cos(teta)*220;Il=220*cos(teta)./L;

>> plot(sin(teta),Ir)

>> grid on

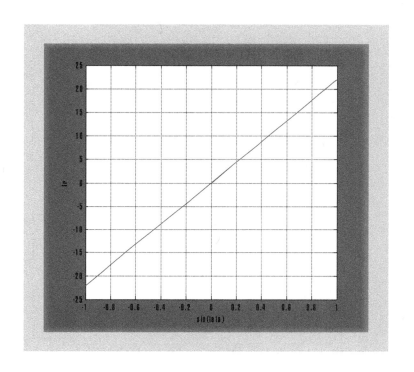

>> teta=0:pi/18:2*pi;

>> V=220*sin(teta);r=10;C=0.0001;L=0.001;

>>Ir=V./r;Ic=C.*cos(teta)*220;Il=220*cos(teta)./L
;

>> plot(sin(teta),Ir)

>> grid on

>> plot(sin(teta),Ic)

>> grid on

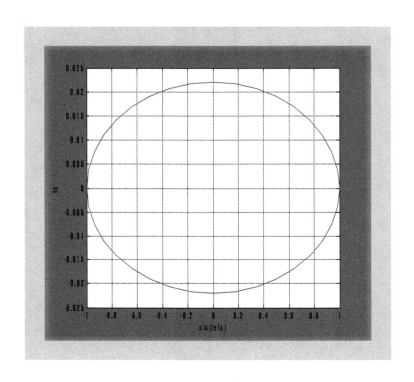

>> teta=0:pi/18:2*pi;

>> V=220*sin(teta);r=10;C=0.0001;L=0.001;

>>Ir=V./r;Ic=C.*cos(teta)*220;Il=220*cos(teta)./L
;

>> plot(sin(teta),Ir)

>> grid on

>> plot(sin(teta),Ic)

>> grid on

>> plot(sin(teta),Il)

>> grid on

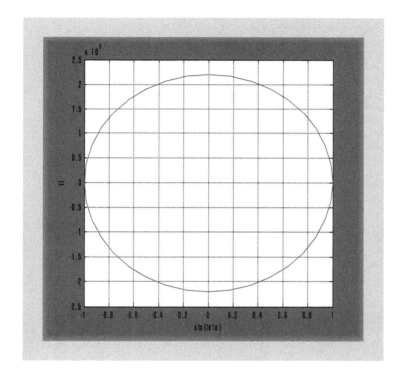

>> teta=0:pi/18:2*pi;

>> V=220*sin(teta);r=10;C=0.0001;L=0.001;

>>Ir=V./r;Ic=C.*cos(teta)*220;Il=220*cos(teta)./;

>> plot(sin(teta),Ir)

```
>> grid on

>> plot(sin(teta),Ic)

>> grid on

>> plot(sin(teta),Il)

>> grid on

>> plot(cos(teta),Ir)

>> grid on
```

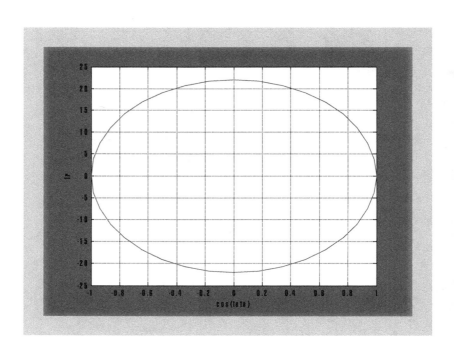

```
>> teta=0:pi/18:2*pi;

>> V=220*sin(teta);r=10;C=0.0001;L=0.001;

>>Ir=V./r;Ic=C.*cos(teta)*220;Il=220*cos(teta)./;

>> plot(sin(teta),Ir)

>> grid on

>> plot(sin(teta),Ic)

>> grid on

>> plot(sin(teta),Il)

>> grid on

>> plot(cos(teta),Ir)

>> grid on

>> plot(cos(teta),Ic)

>> grid on
```

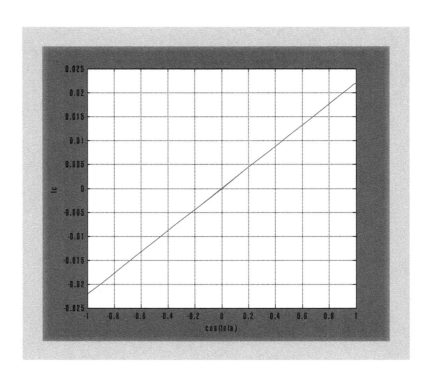

>> teta=0:pi/18:2*pi;

>> V=220*sin(teta);r=10;C=0.0001;L=0.001;

>>Ir=V./r;Ic=C.*cos(teta)*220;Il=220*cos(teta)./;

>> plot(sin(teta),Ir)

>> grid on

>> plot(sin(teta),Ic)

>> grid on

>> plot(sin(teta),Il)

```
>> grid on

>> plot(cos(teta),Ir)

>> grid on

>> plot(cos(teta),Ic)

>> grid on

>> plot(cos(teta),Il)

>> grid on
```

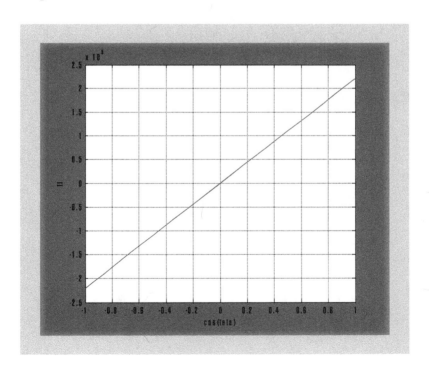

CHAPTER 13

13.0 Plot of trigonometric equations

>> teta=0:pi/18:2*pi;

>> y=sin(2*teta);

>> plot(teta,y)

>> grid on

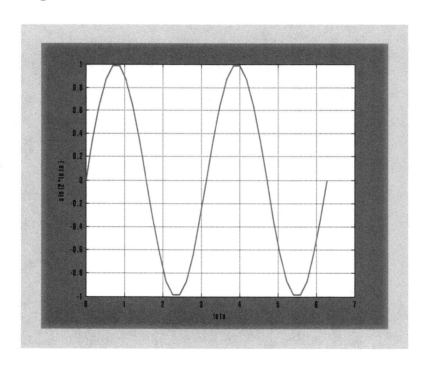

\>> teta=0:pi/18:2*pi;

\>> y=sin(2*teta);

\>> plot(teta,y)

\>> grid on

\>> plot(sin(teta),y)

\>> grid on

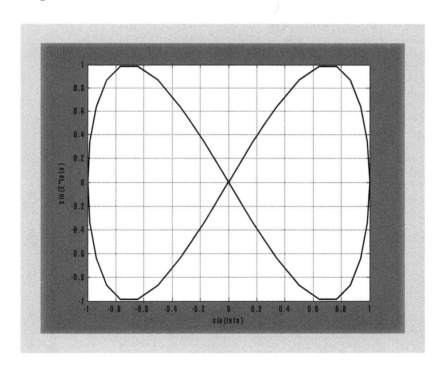

```
>> teta=0:pi/18:2*pi;

>> y=sin(2*teta);

>> plot(teta,y)

>> grid on

>> plot(sin(teta),y)

>> grid on

>> plot(cos(teta),y)

>> grid on
```

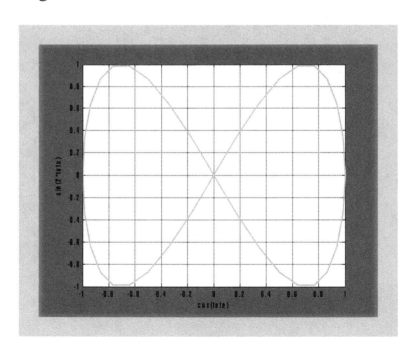

```
>> teta=0:pi/18:2*pi;

>> y=sin(2*teta);

>> plot(teta,y)

>> grid on

>> plot(sin(teta),y)

>> grid on

>> plot(cos(teta),y)

>> grid on

>> plot(tan(teta),y)

>> grid on
```

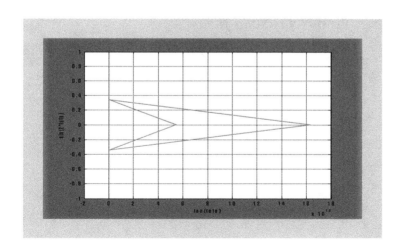

```
>> teta=0:pi/18:2*pi;

>> y=sin(2*teta);

>> plot(teta,y)

>> grid on

>> plot(sin(teta),y)

>> grid on

>> plot(cos(teta),y)

>> grid on

>> plot(tan(teta),y)

>> grid on

>> plot(sin(teta),sin(y))

>> grid on
```

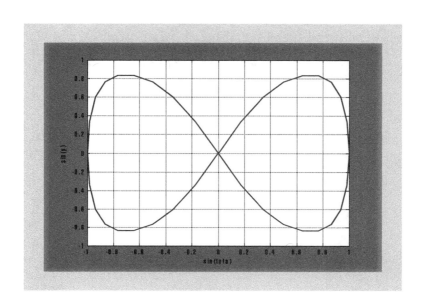

Plot of frequency (s) against transfer function

```
>> s=0.1:0.1:1;

>> R=1./s;

>> G=9./(s.*(s+10));

>> plot(s,R)

>> grid on
```

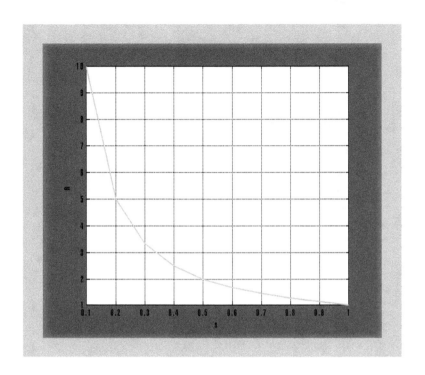

>> s=0.1:0.1:1;

>> R=1./s;

>> G=9./(s.*(s+10));

>> plot(s,R)

>> grid on

>> plot(s,G)

>> grid on

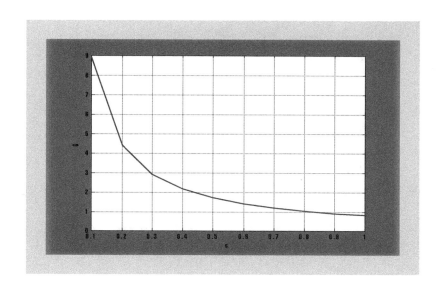

>> s=0.1:0.1:1;

>> R=1./s;

>> G=9./(s.*(s+10));

>> plot(s,R)

>> grid on

>> plot(s,G)

>> grid on

>> plot(R,G)

>> grid on

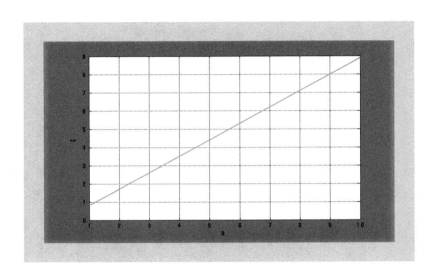

>> s=0.1:0.1:1;

>> R=1./s;

>> G=9./(s+10);

>> H=1;

>> TF=G./(1+G*H)

TF =

 Columns 1 through 6

  0.4712   0.4688   0.4663   0.4639   0.4615
0.4592

Columns 7 through 10

0.4569   0.4545   0.4523   0.4500

>> plot(s,TF)

>> grid on

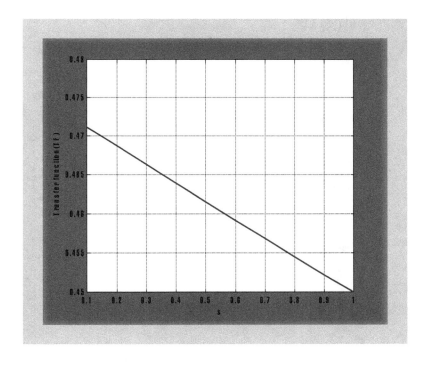

>> s=0.1:0.1:1;

>> R=1./s;

>> G=9./(s+10);

>> H=(s+2);

```
>> TF=G./(1+G*H)
```

??? Error using ==> mtimes

Inner matrix dimensions must agree.

```
>> TF=G./(1+G.*H);
```

```
>> plot(s,TF)
```

```
>> grid on
```

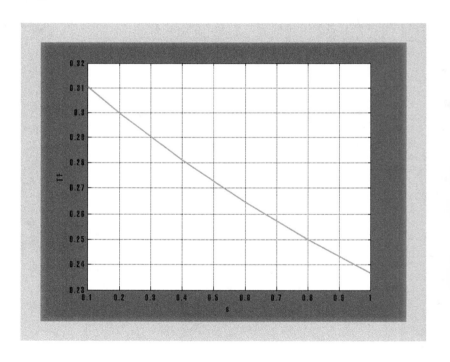

```
>> s=0.1:0.1:1;
```

```
>> R=1./s;
```

```
>> G=9./(s+10);

>> H=(s+2);

>> TF=G./(1+G*H)

??? Error using ==> mtimes

Inner matrix dimensions must agree.

>> TF=G./(1+G.*H);

>> plot(s,TF)

>> grid on

>> plot(R,G)

>> grid on
```

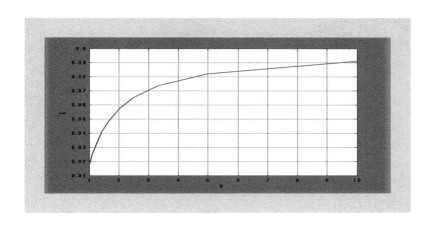

14.0 Use of Subplot

```
s=0:0.1:1;
r=1./(s.^2);
f=1./(r.*(s+1));
plot(s,r,'c');grid on
subplot(2,2,1)
plot(s,f,'m');grid on
subplot(2,2,2)
plot(r,f,'g');grid on
subplot(2,2,3)
plot(1./r,f,'r');grid on
subplot(2,2,4)
```

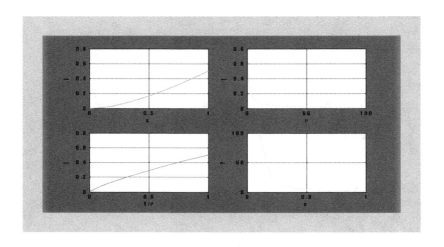

```
s=0:0.01:1;
G=1./(s+1);
R=1./(s.^2);
```

```
T=G.*R;
plot(s,G,'r');grid on
subplot(2,2,1)
plot(s,T,'g');grid on
subplot(2,2,2)
plot(s,R,'c');grid on
subplot(2,2,3)
plot(G,T,'m');grid on
subplot(2,2,4)
```

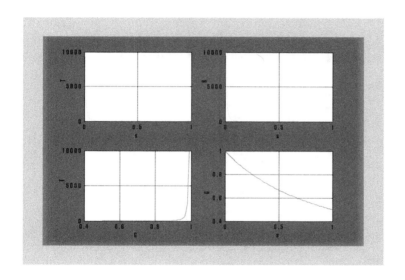

```
s=0:0.01:1;
G=1./(s+1);
R=1./(s.^2);
T=G.*R;
plot(s,G,'r');grid on
subplot(2,3,1)
plot(s,T,'g');grid on
```

```
subplot(2,3,2)
plot(s,R,'c');grid on
subplot(2,3,3)
plot(G,T,'m');grid on
subplot(2,3,4)
plot(1./s,G,'b');grid on
subplot(2,3,5)
plot(1./s,T,'k');grid on
subplot(2,3,6)
```

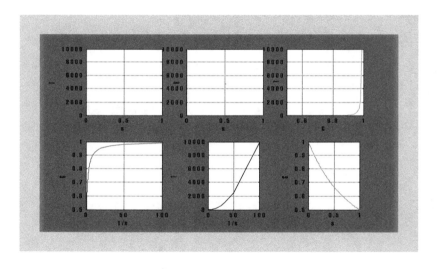

```
s=0:0.01:1;
z=1./(s+3);
A=1./s.^2;
D=A.*z;
plot(s,z,'r',s,A,'g',s,D,'c',A,D,'m');grid on
```

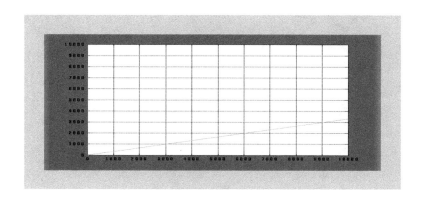

>> s=0.1:0.1:1;

>> G=14000/(s.^3+45*s.^2+3100.*s+14500)

??? Error using ==> mrdivide

Matrix dimensions must agree.

>> G=14000/(s.^3+45.*s.^2+3100.*s+14500);

??? Error using ==> mrdivide

Matrix dimensions must agree.

>> G=14000./(s.^3+45*s.^2+3100.*s+14500);

>> plot(s,G)

>> grid on

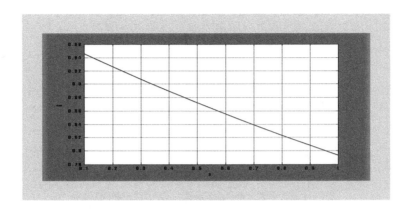

188

CHAPTER 14

14.0 PLOT OF VELOCITY AGAINST KINETIC ENERGY

>> v=0:2:10;

>> m=10;

>> E=m.*v.^2./2;

>> plot(v,E)

>> grid on

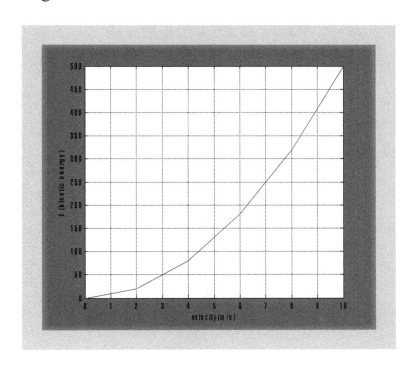

```
>> v=0:2:10;

>> m=10;

>> E=m.*v.^2./2;

>> plot(v,E)

>> grid on

>> plot(v,log(E))

>> grid on
```

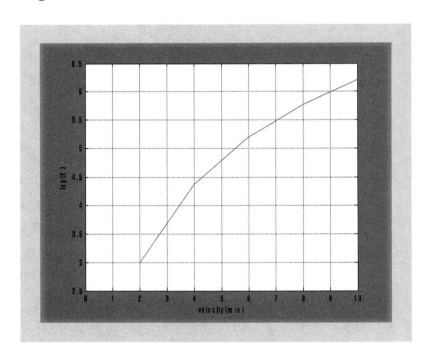

Plot of height against potential energy

```
>> v=0:2:10;

>> m=10;

>> g=10;

>> E=m*g*h;

>> Ep=m*g*h;

>> plot(h,Ep)

>> grid on
```

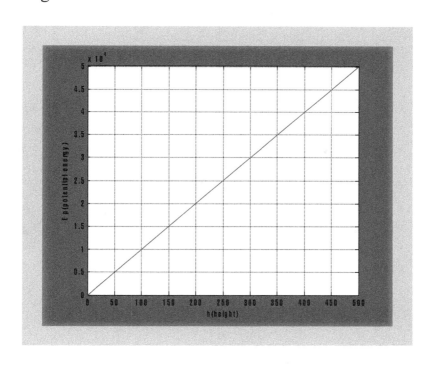

```
>> v=0:2:10;

>> m=10;

>> g=10;

>> E=m*g*h;

>> Ep=m*g*h;

>> plot(h,Ep)

>> grid on

>> plot(h,log(Ep))

>> grid on
```

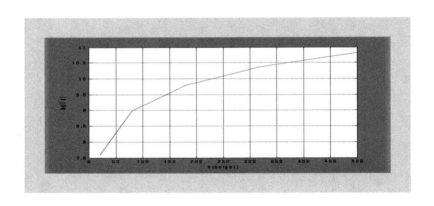

Plot of two quantities (kinetic energy and potential energy) against velocity

```
>> v=0:2:10;

>> m=10;

>> g=10;

>> h=v.^2/2*g;

>> Ep=m*g*h;

>> E=m.*v.^2./2;

>> plot(v,E,Ep);grid on

??? Error using ==> plot
```

Data must be a single matrix Y or a list of pairs X,Y

```
>> plot(v,E,v,Ep);grid on
```

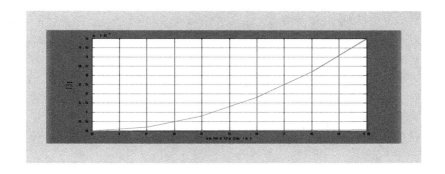

15.0 USE OF m-FILE

Enter the parameters on the m-file window or command window. You can use the command window as checks to the execution of the parameters.

Using the plot command;

Plot(x,y,'g');grid on

where x refers to the parameter to be plotted on x-axis.

y refers to the parameters to be plotted on y-axis.

and g refers to the color to be used for the plotting.

Subplot;

You can use this command if you want to plot series of graphs on a sheet.

Example;

Subplot(2,1,1) will produce two graphs in one sheet. The first two numbers i.e 2 and 1 indicate that the maximum possible plots in one sheet is

2.

Subplot(2,2,1) will produce four graphs in one sheet.

Subplot(2,3,1) will produce 6 graphs in one sheet.

Possible values of subplot(2,1,1);

Subplot(2,1,1)

Subplot(2,1,2)

Possible values of subplot(2,2,1);

Subplot(2,2,1)

Subplot(2,2,2)

Subplot(2,2,3)

Subplot(2,2,4).

Possible values of subplot(2,3,1)

Subplot(2,3,1)

Subplot(2,3,2)

Subplot(2,3,3)

Subplot(2,3,4)

Subplot(2,3,5)

Subplot(2,3,6).

Double click the play sign on the m-file menu to display the graphs.

Click on a particular graph to insert the values. Click on insert menu to insert the values on the plotted graph.

Click on edit menu to copy figure.

The available colors on matlab are as follow;

Color strings are 'c', 'm', 'y', 'r', 'g', 'b', 'w', and 'k'. These correspond

to cyan, magenta, yellow, red, green, blue, white, and black.

Examples;

```
>> v=0:2:10;

>> m=10;

>> g=10;

>> h=v.^2/2*g;

>> Ep=m*g*h;

>> E=m.*v.^2./2;

>> plot(v,E);grid on

>> subplot(2,2,1)

>> plot(v,Ep);grid on

>> subplot(2,2,2)

>> plot(h,Ep);grid on

>> subplot(2,2,3)

>> plot(v,log(E));grid on

>> subplot(2,2,4)
```

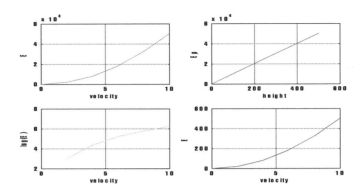

>> s=0:0.1:1;

>> Hs=(s+2);

>> Gs=(9./(s+10));

>> Rs=(1./s);

>> Cs=((Gs.*Rs)./(1+Gs.*Hs));

>> plot(s,Cs);grid on

>> subplot(2,2,1)

>> plot(s,Rs);grid on

>> subplot(2,2,2)

>> plot(s,Hs);grid on

>> subplot(2,2,3)

>> plot(s,Gs);grid on

>> subplot(2,2,4)

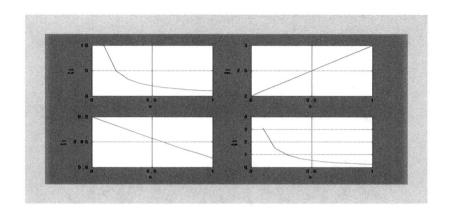

>> s=0:0.1:1;

>> Hs=(s+2);

>> Gs=(9./(s+10));

>> Rs=(1./s);

>> Cs=((Gs.*Rs)./(1+Gs.*Hs));

>> plot(s,Cs);grid on

>> subplot(2,1,1)

>> plot(s,Rs);grid on

>> subplot(2,1,2)

>> plot(s,Rs);grid on

>> subplot(2,1,3)

??? Error using ==> subplot at 276

Index exceeds number of subplots.

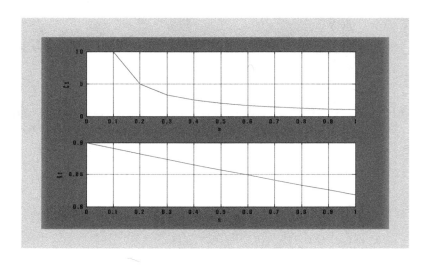

>> s=0:0.1:1;

>> Hs=(s+2);

>> Gs=(9./(s+10));

>> Rs=(1./s);

>> Cs=((Gs.*Rs)./(1+Gs.*Hs));

>> plot(s,Cs);grid on

>> subplot(2,3,1)

```
>> plot(s,Hs);grid on

>> subplot(2,3,2)

>> plot(s,Gs);grid on

>> subplot(2,3,3)

>> plot(s,Rs);grid on

>> subplot(2,3,4)

>> plot(Hs,Gs);grid on

>> subplot(2,3,5)

>> plot(Hs,Cs);grid on

>> subplot(2,3,6)

>> plot(Rs,Cs);grid on

>> subplot(2,3,7)

??? Error using ==> subplot at 276

Index exceeds number of subplots.
```

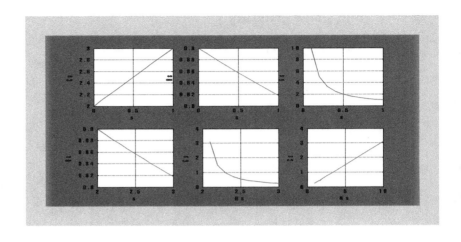

```
s=0:0.1:1;
Hs=(s+2);
Gs=(9./(s+10));
Rs=(1./s);
Cs=((Gs.*Rs)./(1+Gs.*Hs));
plot(s,Cs,'r');grid on
subplot(2,3,1)
plot(s,Hs,'g');grid on
subplot(2,3,2)
plot(s,Gs,'y');grid on
subplot(2,3,3)
plot(s,Rs,'b');grid on
subplot(2,3,4)
plot(Hs,Gs,'gr');grid on
subplot(2,3,5)
plot(Hs,Cs,'bl');grid on
subplot(2,3,6)
```

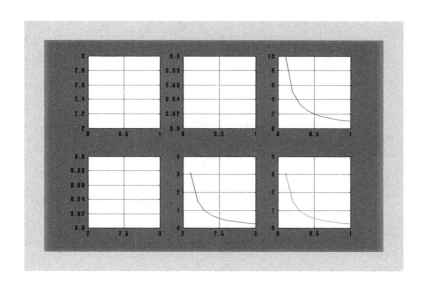

>> teta=0:pi/18:2*pi;

>> y=sin(2*teta);

>> plot(teta,y,'c');grid on

>> subplot(2,2,1)

>> plot(sin(teta),sin(y),'m');grid on

>> subplot(2,2,2)

>> plot(sin(teta),cos(y),'k');grid on

>> subplot(2,2,3)

>> plot(cos(teta),sin(y),'r');grid on

>> subplot(2,2,4)

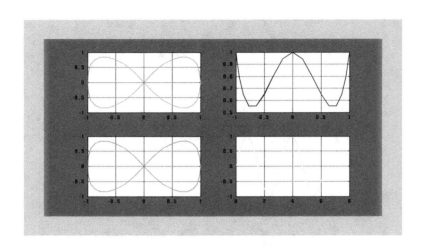

```
teta=0:pi/18:2*pi;
y=sin(2*teta);
plot(teta,cos(y),'b');grid on
subplot(2,1,1)
plot(cos(teta),cos(y),'g');grid on
subplot(2,1,2)
```

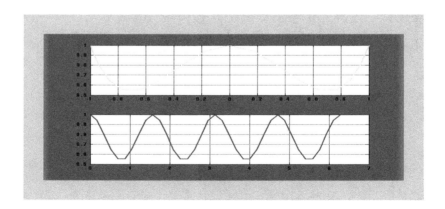

CHAPTER 15

15.0 DETERMINATION OF ACTIVE, REACTIVE AND APPARENT POWERS

```
>> v=0:10:450;

>> va=1.732.*v*10;

>> teta=(pi/4);

>> w=va*(cos(teta));

>> pf=cos(teta);

>> Pin=1.732.*v*10*pf;

>> Pout=3750;

>> eff=(Pout./Pin);

>> plot(v,eff,'r');grid on

>> subplot(2,2,1)

>> plot(Pin,eff,'k');grid on

>> subplot(2,2,2)

>> plot(v,pf,'b');grid on

>> subplot(2,2,3)
```

```
>> plot(v,w,'m');grid on

>> subplot(2,2,4)
```

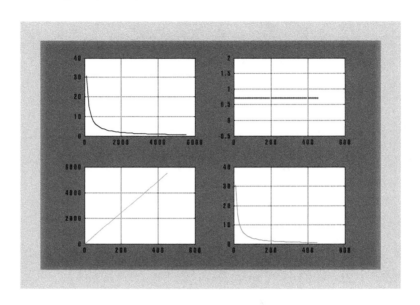

```
>> teta=0:pi/18:2*pi;

>> pf=cos(teta);

>> Pin=1.732*415*10.*pf;

>> Pout=3750;

>> eff=(Pout./Pin);

>> plot(teta,eff,'g');grid on

>> subplot(2,2,1)
```

\>> plot(pf,eff,'k');grid on

\>> subplot(2,2,2)

\>> plot(Pin,eff,'r');grid on

\>> subplot(2,2,3)

\>> plot(sin(pf),eff,'m');grid on

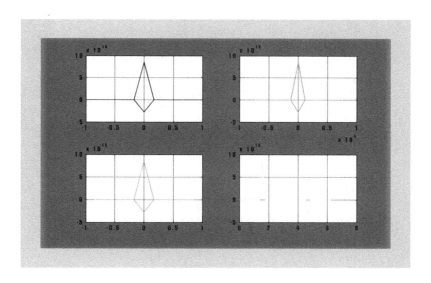

teta=0:pi/18:2*pi;

\>> pf=cos(teta);

\>> Pin=1.732*415*10.*pf;

\>> Pout=3750;

\>> plot(sin(teta),pf,'r');grid on

```
>> subplot(2,1,1)

>> plot(sin(teta),eff,'g');grid on

>> subplot(2,1,2)
```

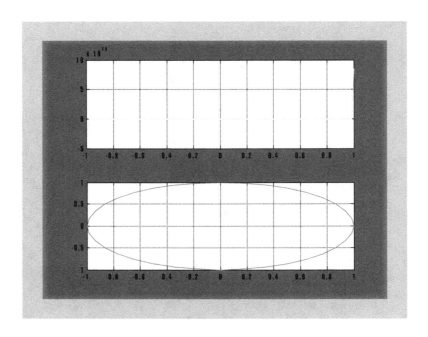

```
>> w=0:100:1800;

>> T=(3*P./w);

>> plot(w,T,'g');grid on

>> subplot(2,2,1)

>> plot(w,1./T,'c');grid on

>> subplot(2,2,2)
```

```
>> plot(w,log(1./T),'r');grid on

>> subplot(2,2,3)

>> plot(1./w,1./T,'m');grid on

>> subplot(2,2,4)
```

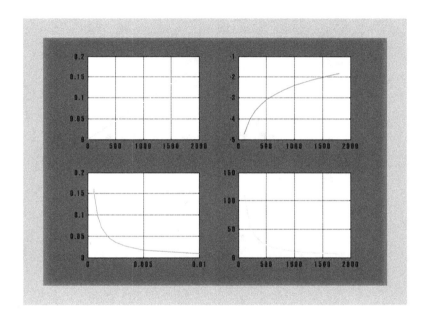

```
s=0.01:0.1:1;
f=50;
t=1;
w=2*pi*f*t;
we=(1-s)*w;
plot(s,we,'g');grid on
subplot(2,2,1)
plot(s,log(we),'r');grid on
```

```
subplot(2,2,2)
plot(log(s),log(we),'g');grid on
subplot(2,2,3)
plot(log(s),we,'m');grid on
subplot(2,2,4)
```

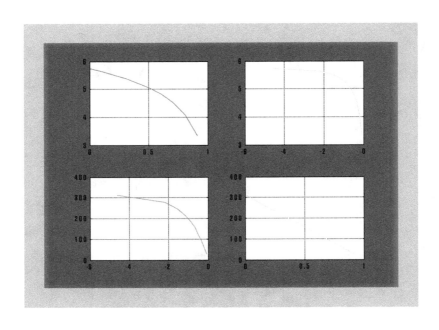

```
>> x=0:2:10;

>> y=x+2;

>> plot(x,y,'r');grid on

>> subplot(2,2,1)

>> plot(x,log(y),'c');grid on

>> subplot(2,2,2)
```

```
>> plot(1./x,1./y,'k');grid on

>> subplot(2,2,3)

>> plot(log(x),log(y),'m');grid on

>> subplot(2,2,4)
```

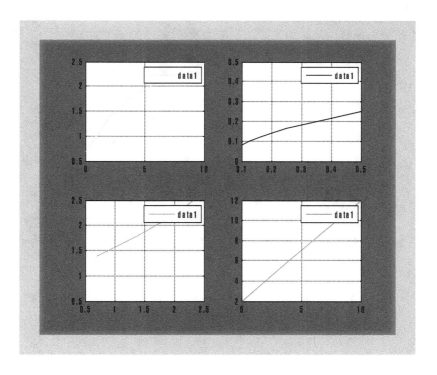

```
i=10;s=0.03;r=0.2;
T=(3*i^2*r)./(s.*w);
plot(w,T,'r');grid on
subplot(2,2,1)
plot(w,log(T),'y');grid on
subplot(2,2,2)
```

```
plot(w,1./T,'k');grid on
subplot(2,2,3)
plot(1./w,1./T,'m');grid on
subplot(2,2,4)
```

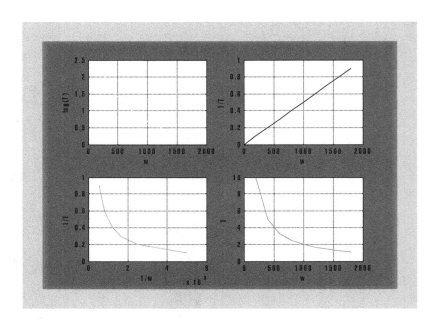

```
w=0:200:1800;
i=10;s=0.03;r=0.2;
T=(3*i^2*r)./(s.*w*(1-s));
plot(w,T,'r');grid on
subplot(2,2,1)
plot(w,log(T),'y');grid on
subplot(2,2,2)
plot(w,1./T,'k');grid on
subplot(2,2,3)
plot(1./w,1./T,'m');grid on
subplot(2,2,4)
```

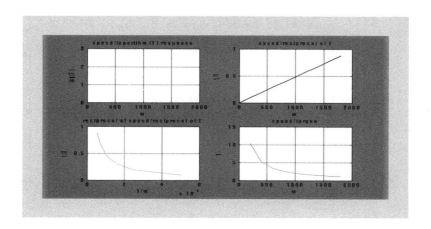

```
s=-1:0.1:2;
Pm=10;w=1500;
T=Pm./(s*w);
plot(s,T,'r');grid on
subplot(2,1,1)
plot(s,log(T),'m');grid on
subplot(2,1,2)
```

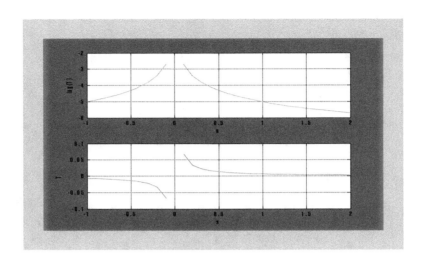

```
w=-1500:100:1500;
Pm=10;s=0.05;
T=Pm./(s*w);
plot(w,T,'r');grid on
subplot(2,1,1)
plot(w,log(T),'m');grid on
subplot(2,1,2)
```

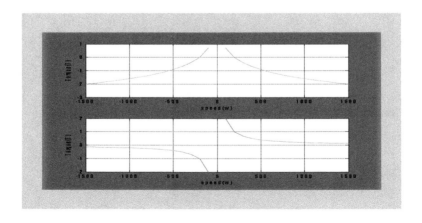

```
Pm=0:150:7500;
w=1500;s=0.05;
T=Pm./(s*w);
plot(Pm,T,'r');grid on
subplot(2,1,1)
plot(Pm,log(T),'m');grid on
subplot(2,1,2)
```

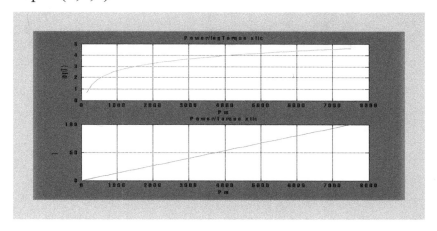

```
s=0:0.1:1;
rs=0.2;rr=0.02;Xm=10.05;Xs=0.5;Xr=0.05;rm=2;i
=10;
Rt=rs+rr./s+Xs+Xr./s+((Xm*rm)/(Xm+rm));
V=Rt*i;
plot(s,Rt,'g');grid on
subplot(2,1,1)
plot(Rt,V,'m');grid on
subplot(2,1,2)
```

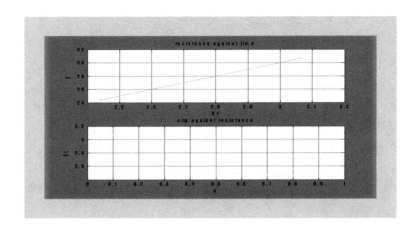

CHAPTER 16

16.0 ELECTRICAL MACHINE PARAMETERS

```
teta=-2*pi:pi/18:2*pi;
E=415;
V=300;
X=10;
P=(3*V*E./X)*sin(teta);
Q=(3*V*E./X)*cos(teta)-(3*V*V./X);
plot(teta,P,'g');grid on
subplot(2,3,1)
plot(sin(teta),P,'r');grid on
subplot(2,3,2)
plot(cos(teta),P,'m');grid on
subplot(2,3,3)
plot(cos(teta),Q,'y');grid on
subplot(2,3,4)
plot(sin(teta),Q,'k');grid on
subplot(2,3,5)
plot(teta,P./Q,'c');grid on
subplot(2,3,6)
```

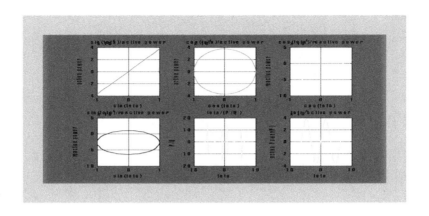

```
Is=0:0.1:5;
Lm=10;Ls=0.01;Lr=0.001;w=314;rr=0.2;
Xm=w.*Lm;Xs=w.*Ls;Xr=w.*Lr;Zs=Xm+Xs+Xr
+rr;
Vs=Is.*Zs;
Pm=3.*Is.^2.*Zs;
T=(3.*Pm.*Is.^2.*rr)./2.*w;
plot(Is,Pm,'r');grid on
subplot(2,3,1)
plot(Is,Vs,'g');grid on
subplot(2,3,2)
plot(Is,Zs,'c');grid on
subplot(2,3,3)
plot(Is,T,'k');grid on
subplot(2,3,4)
plot(Pm,T,'y');grid on
subplot(2,3,5)
plot(Zs,T,'m');grid on
subplot(2,3,6)
```

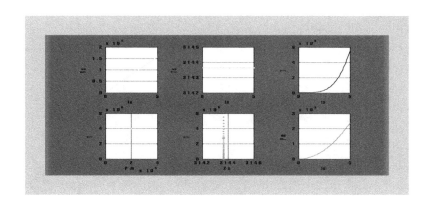

```
Is=0:0.1:5;
Lm=10;Ls=0.01;Lr=0.001;w=314;rr=0.2;
Xm=w.*Lm;Xs=w.*Ls;Xr=w.*Lr;Zs=Xm+Xs+Xr
+rr;
Vs=Is.*Zs;
Pm=3.*Is.^2.*Zs;
T=(3.*Pm.*Is.^2.*rr)./2.*w;
plot(Is,Pm,'r');grid on
subplot(2,3,1)
plot(Is,Vs,'g');grid on
subplot(2,3,2)
plot(Is,Pm./T,'c');grid on
subplot(2,3,3)
plot(Is,T,'k');grid on
subplot(2,3,4)
plot(Pm,T,'y');grid on
subplot(2,3,5)
plot(Vs,T,'m');grid on
subplot(2,3,6)
```

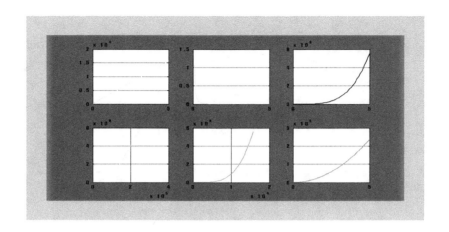

```
Lm=0.035;rs=0.3;rr=15;Lls=0.0015;Llr=0.0007;p=
2;w=377;s=0:0.1:1;
we=(2./p)*w;Xm=w*Lm;Xls=w*Lls;Xlr=w*Llr;V
as=208/3^0.5;
Za=Xm*(Xlr+rr./s);
Zb=(Xlr+rr./s)+Xm;
Zr=Za./Zb;
Zs=rs+Xls+Zr;
Ias=Vas./Zs;
Iar=(Ias*Xm)./(Xlr+rr./s+Xm);
Pm=3.*Iar.^2.*rr.*(1-s)./s;
T=(3.*Pm.*Iar.^2.*rr)./2.*w.*s;
wr=(1-s)*we;
N=(60*wr)/2*pi;
plot(wr,T,'g');grid on
subplot(2,3,1)
plot(wr,Iar,'k');grid on
subplot(2,3,2)
plot(Pm,T,'r');grid on
```

```
subplot(2,3,3)
plot(Iar,T,'c');grid on
subplot(2,3,4)
plot(s,N,'m');grid on
subplot(2,3,5)
plot(Iar,Pm,'y');grid on
subplot(2,3,6)
```

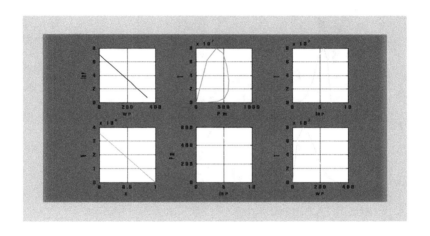

```
n=-1500:100:1500;
s=0.05;i=10;r=0.2;P=3750;
T=3*i^2*r.*(1-s)./(s.*n);
plot(n,T,'k');grid on
subplot(2,2,1)
plot(n,1./T,'r');grid on
subplot(2,2,2)
plot(log(n),log(T),'m');grid on
subplot(2,2,3)
plot(1./n,1./T,'y');grid on
```

subplot(2,2,4)

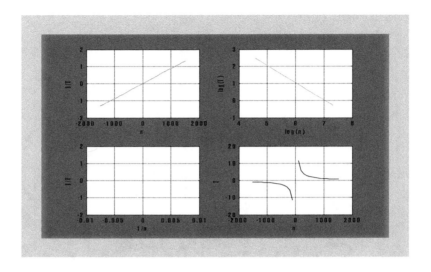

```
n=0:200:3000;
s=0.05;i=10;r=0.2;P=3750;
T=3*i^2*r.*(1-s)./(s.*n);
plot(n,T,'k');grid on
subplot(2,2,1)
plot(n,1./T,'r');grid on
subplot(2,2,2)
plot(log(n),log(T),'m');grid on
subplot(2,2,3)
plot(1./n,1./T,'y');grid on
subplot(2,2,4)
```

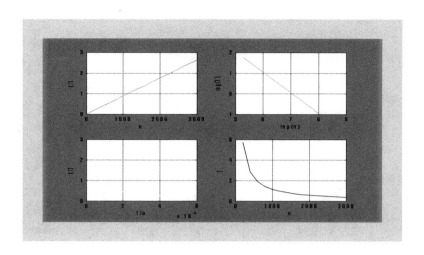

```
teta=-150:10:150;
i=10;Pout=7500;
v=415;
pf=cos(teta);
Pin=1.732*i*v.*pf;
eff=Pout./Pin;
plot(teta,pf,'k');grid on
subplot(2,2,1)
plot(eff,pf,'r');grid on
subplot(2,2,2)
plot(pf,Pin,'y');grid on
subplot(2,2,3)
plot(eff,Pin,'m');grid on
subplot(2,2,4)
```

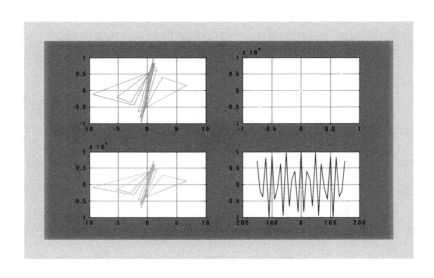

```
teta=-5*pi/6:pi/18:5*pi/6;
i=10;Pout=7500;
v=415;
pf=cos(teta);
Pin=1.732*i*v.*pf;
eff=Pout./Pin;
plot(teta,pf,'k');grid on
subplot(2,2,1)
plot(pf,eff,'r');grid on
subplot(2,2,2)
plot(pf,Pin,'y');grid on
subplot(2,2,3)
plot(Pin,eff,'m');grid on
subplot(2,2,4)
```

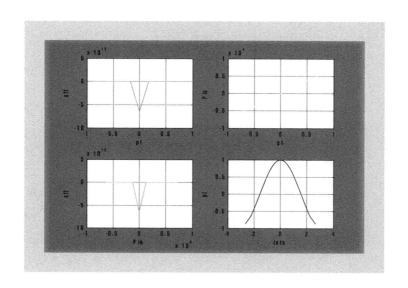

```
teta=-5*pi/6:pi/18:5*pi/6;
i=10;Pout=7500;
v=415;
pf=cos(teta);
Pin=1.732*i*v.*pf;
eff=Pout./Pin;
plot(teta,pf,'k');grid on
subplot(2,3,1)
plot(pf,eff,'r');grid on
subplot(2,3,2)
plot(pf,Pin,'y');grid on
subplot(2,3,3)
plot(Pin,eff,'m');grid on
subplot(2,3,4)
plot(1./pf,1./eff,'g');grid on
subplot(2,3,5)
plot(teta,eff,'c');grid on
```

225

subplot(2,3,6)

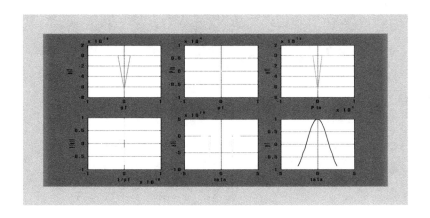

```
teta=0:pi/18:5*pi/6;
i=10;Pout=7500;
v=415;
pf=cos(teta);
Pin=1.732*i*v.*pf;
eff=Pout./Pin;
plot(teta,pf,'k');grid on
subplot(2,3,1)
plot(pf,eff,'r');grid on
subplot(2,3,2)
plot(pf,Pin,'y');grid on
subplot(2,3,3)
plot(Pin,eff,'m');grid on
subplot(2,3,4)
plot(1./pf,1./eff,'g');grid on
subplot(2,3,5)
```

```
plot(teta,eff,'c');grid on
subplot(2,3,6)
```

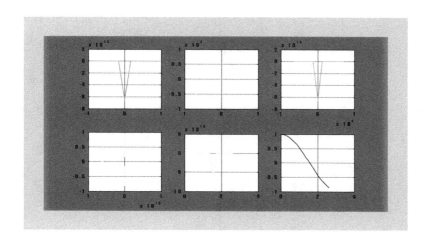

```
v=0:50:500;
i=10;Pout=7500;
teta=pi/4;
pf=cos(teta);
Pin=1.732*i.*v*pf;
eff=Pout./Pin;
plot(v,(1-eff),'k');grid on
subplot(2,3,1)
plot(v,eff,'r');grid on
subplot(2,3,2)
plot(v,Pin,'y');grid on
subplot(2,3,3)
plot(Pin,eff,'m');grid on
subplot(2,3,4)
plot(1./v,1./eff,'g');grid on
subplot(2,3,5)
```

```
plot(1./v,eff,'c');grid on
subplot(2,3,6)
```

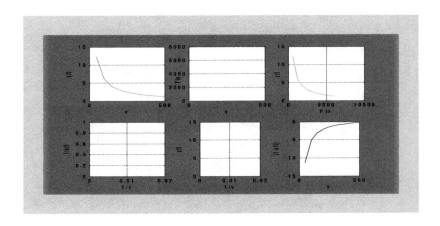

```
v=0:50:500;
i=10;Pout=7500;
teta=pi/18;
pf=cos(teta);
Pin=1.732*i.*v*pf;
eff=Pout./Pin;
plot(v,(1-eff),'k');grid on
subplot(2,3,1)
plot(v,eff,'r');grid on
subplot(2,3,2)
plot(v,Pin,'y');grid on
subplot(2,3,3)
plot(Pin,eff,'m');grid on
subplot(2,3,4)
plot(1./v,1./eff,'g');grid on
subplot(2,3,5)
plot(1./v,eff,'c');grid on
```

subplot(2,3,6)

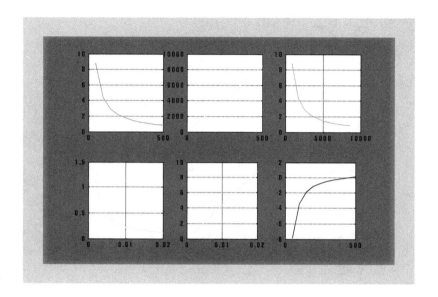

```
teta=0:pi/18:pi/4;
i=10;Pout=7500;
v=415;
pf=cos(teta);
Pin=1.732*i.*v*pf;
eff=Pout./Pin;
plot(pf,(1-eff),'k');grid on
subplot(2,3,1)
plot(teta,eff,'r');grid on
subplot(2,3,2)
plot(pf,Pin,'y');grid on
subplot(2,3,3)
plot(Pin,eff,'m');grid on
subplot(2,3,4)
```

```
plot(sin(teta),eff,'g');grid on
subplot(2,3,5)
plot(pf,eff,'c');grid on
subplot(2,3,6)
```

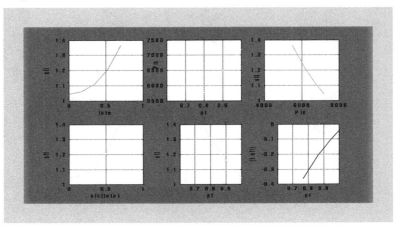

```
teta=0:pi/18:pi/4;
i=10;Pout=7500;
v=208;
pf=cos(teta);
Pin=1.732*i.*v*pf;
eff=Pout./Pin;
plot(tan(teta),eff,'k');grid on
subplot(2,3,1)
plot(teta,eff,'r');grid on
subplot(2,3,2)
plot(pf,Pin,'y');grid on
subplot(2,3,3)
plot(Pin,eff,'m');grid on
subplot(2,3,4)
plot(sin(teta),eff,'g');grid on
```

```
subplot(2,3,5)
plot(pf,eff,'c');grid on
subplot(2,3,6)
```

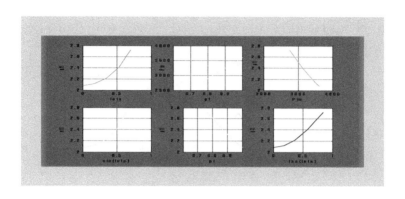

```
s=-1:0.1:1;r=0.5;i=10;n=1500;
w=n*pi/30;
T=3*i*2*r.*(1-s)./(w.*s);
plot(s,T,'b');grid on
subplot(2,1,1)
plot(1./s,1./T,'g');grid on
subplot(2,1,2)
```

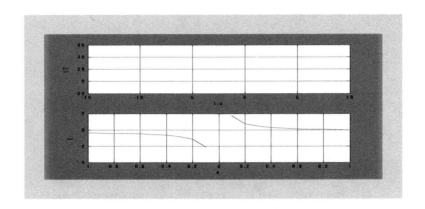

s=0:0.1:1;r=0.5;i=10;n=1500;
w=n*pi/30;
T=3*i^2*r.*(1-s)./(w.*s);
plot(s,T,'b');grid on
subplot(2,1,1)
plot(1./s,1./T,'g');grid on
subplot(2,1,2)

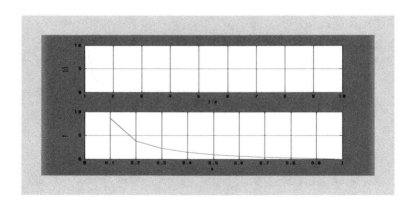

232

```
s=0:0.1:1;r=0.5;i=10;n=1500;
w=n*pi/30;
nr=n.*(1-s)./s;
T=3*i^2*r.*(1-s)./(w.*s);
plot(s,T,'b');grid on
subplot(2,2,1)
plot(s,nr,'g');grid on
subplot(2,2,2)
plot(nr,T,'r');grid on
subplot(2,2,3)
plot(1./nr,1./T,'k');grid on
subplot(2,2,4)
```

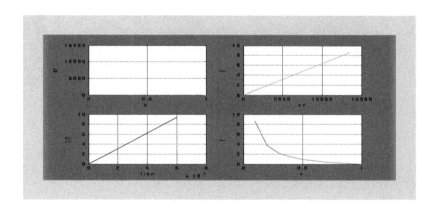

```
s=0:0.1:1;r=0.5;i=10;n=1500;
w=n*pi/30;
nr=n.*(1-s)./s;
T=3*i^2*r.*(1-s)./(w.*s);
plot(s,T,'b');grid on
subplot(2,2,1)
plot(s,nr,'g');grid on
```

```
subplot(2,2,2)
plot(nr.*s,T,'r');grid on
subplot(2,2,3)
plot(1./nr,1./T,'k');grid on
subplot(2,2,4)
```

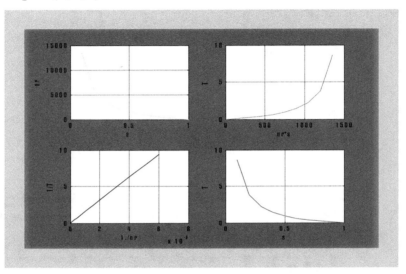

```
s=0:0.1:1;r=0.5;i=10;n=1500;
w=n*pi/30;
nr=n.*(1-s)./s;
T=3*i^2*r.*(1-s)./(w.*s);
plot(s,T,'b');grid on
subplot(2,2,1)
plot(s,nr,'g');grid on
subplot(2,2,2)
plot(1./s,nr.*T,'r');grid on
subplot(2,2,3)
plot(1./nr,1./T,'k');grid on
subplot(2,2,4)
```

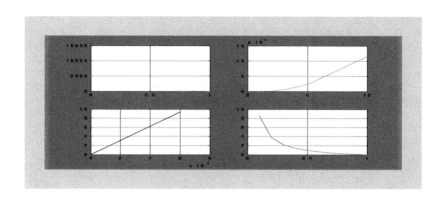

```
s=-3:0.1:4;
wn=1;
zeta=1;
D=s.^2+2.*s*wn*(zeta)+wn^2;
plot(s,D,'k');grid on
subplot(2,1,1)
plot(s,1./D,'g');grid on
subplot(2,1,2)
```

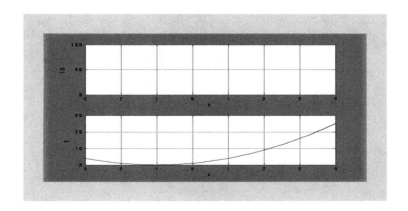

```
s=-3:0.1:4;
wn=1;
zeta=1;
D=s.^2+2.*s*wn*(zeta)+wn^2;
plot(s,D,'k');grid on
subplot(2,2,1)
plot(s,1./D,'g');grid on
subplot(2,2,2)
plot(i./s,D,'y');grid on
subplot(2,2,3)
plot(1./s,1./D,'b');grid on
subplot(2,2,4)
```

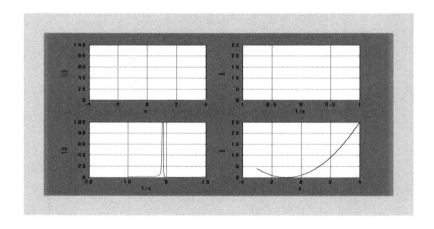

```
s=-3:0.1:4;
wn=1;
zeta=1;
D=s.^2+2.*s*wn*(zeta)+wn^2;
plot(s,D,'k');grid on
```

```
subplot(2,2,1)
plot(s,1./D,'g');grid on
subplot(2,2,2)
plot(s,D.*s,'y');grid on
subplot(2,2,3)
plot(1./s,1./D,'b');grid on
subplot(2,2,4)
```

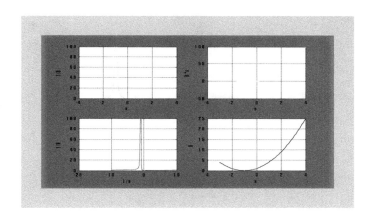

```
s=-4:0.1:4;
Rs=1./s;
Ds=(s+1).*Rs./(s.^3+3.*s.^2+3.*s+1);
plot(s,Ds,'b');grid on
subplot(2,2,1)
plot(s,Rs,'k');grid on
subplot(2,2,2)
plot(Rs,Ds,'y');grid on
subplot(2,2,3)
plot(s,Rs./Ds,'m');grid on
subplot(2,2,4)
```

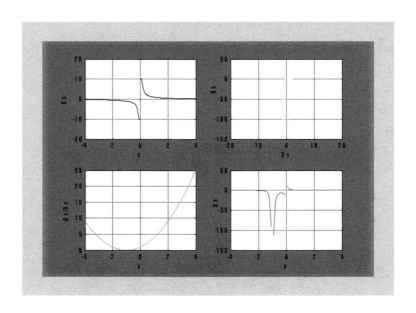

```
s=-4:0.1:4;
Rs=1./s.^2;
Ds=(s+1).*Rs./(s.^3+3.*s.^2+3.*s+1);
plot(s,Ds,'b');grid on
subplot(2,2,1)
plot(s,Rs,'k');grid on
subplot(2,2,2)
plot(Rs,Ds,'y');grid on
subplot(2,2,3)
plot(s,Rs./Ds,'m');grid on
subplot(2,2,4)
```

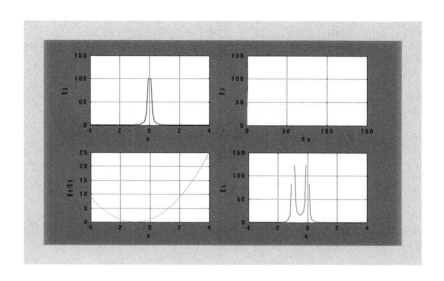

```
s=-4:0.1:4;
Rs=s;
Ds=(s+1).*Rs./(s.^3+3.*s.^2+3.*s+1);
plot(s,Ds,'b');grid on
subplot(2,2,1)
plot(s,Rs,'k');grid on
subplot(2,2,2)
plot(Rs,Ds,'y');grid on
subplot(2,2,3)
plot(s,Rs./Ds,'m');grid on
subplot(2,2,4)
```

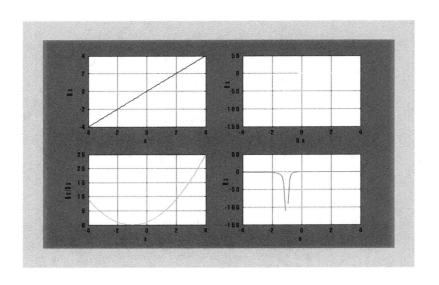

```
s=-4:0.1:4;
Rs=s;
Ds=(s+1).*Rs./(s.^3+3.*s.^2+3.*s+1);
plot(s,Ds,'b');grid on
subplot(2,2,1)
plot(s,Rs,'k');grid on
subplot(2,2,2)
plot(Rs,1./Ds,'y');grid on
subplot(2,2,3)
plot(s,Ds./Rs,'m');grid on
subplot(2,2,4)
```

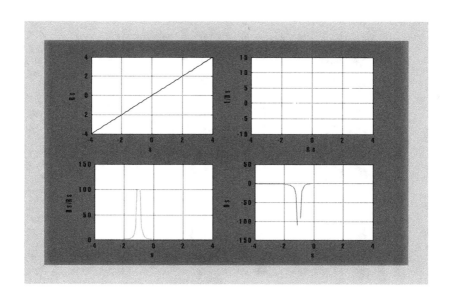

```
s=-4:0.1:4;
Rs=s;
Ds=(s+1).*Rs./(s.^3+3.*s.^2+3.*s+1);
plot(1./s,Ds,'b');grid on
subplot(2,2,1)
plot(1./s,Rs,'k');grid on
subplot(2,2,2)
plot(s.*Rs,s./Ds,'r');grid on
subplot(2,2,3)
plot(1./s,Ds./Rs,'m');grid on
subplot(2,2,4)
```

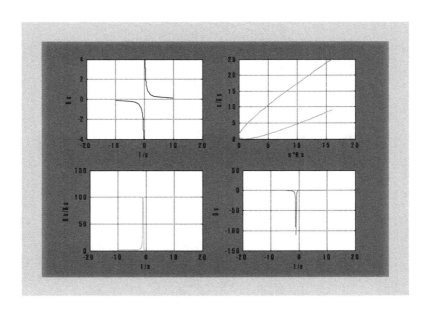

```
s=-4:0.1:4;
Rs=1./s.^2;
Ds=(s+1).*Rs./(s.^3+3.*s.^2+3.*s+1);
plot(s,1./Ds,'b');grid on
subplot(2,2,1)
plot(1./s,Rs,'k');grid on
subplot(2,2,2)
plot(s.*Rs,s./Ds,'r');grid on
subplot(2,2,3)
plot(1./s,Ds./Rs,'m');grid on
subplot(2,2,4)
```

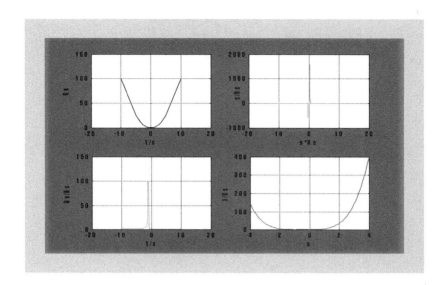

CHAPTER 16

16.0 ACTIVE AND REACTIVE POWERS

```
teta=0:pi/18:pi/2;
i=8;
v=415;
P=i*v.*cos(teta);
Q=i*v.*sin(teta);
S=P+j*Q;
pf=cos(teta);
Pin= 1.732.*v*i*pf;
plot(pf,P,'r');grid on
subplot(2,3,1)
plot(pf,Q,'g');grid on
subplot(2,3,2)
plot(pf,S,'k');grid on
subplot(2,3,3)
plot(P,S,'b');grid on
subplot(2,3,4)
plot(Q,S,'c');grid on
subplot(2,3,5)
plot(P,Q,'m');grid on
subplot(2,3,6)
```

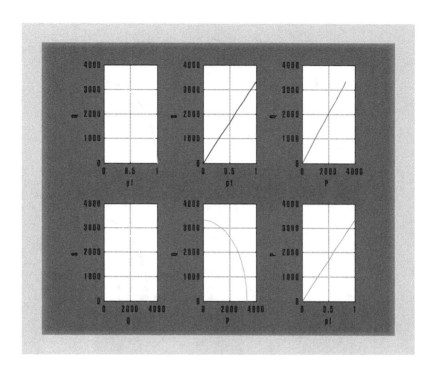

```
teta=0:pi/18:pi/2;
i=8;
v=415;
P=i*v.*cos(teta);
Q=i*v.*sin(teta);
S=P+j*Q;
pf=cos(teta);
Pin= 1.732.*v*i*pf;
plot(pf,P./Q,'r');grid on
subplot(2,3,1)
plot(teta,P,'g');grid on
subplot(2,3,2)
plot(teta,S,'k');grid on
```

```
subplot(2,3,3)
plot(P,S,'b');grid on
subplot(2,3,4)
plot(Q,S,'c');grid on
subplot(2,3,5)
plot(teta,Q,'m');grid on
subplot(2,3,6)
```

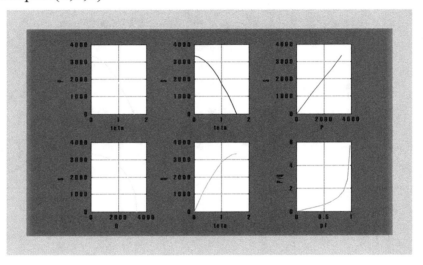

```
teta=0:pi/18:pi/2;
i=8;
v=415;
P=i*v.*cos(teta);
Q=i*v.*sin(teta);
S=P+j*Q;
pf=cos(teta);
Pin= 1.732.*v*i*pf;
plot(pf,P./Q,'r');grid on
subplot(2,3,1)
```

```
plot(teta,P./Q,'g');grid on
subplot(2,3,2)
plot(teta,S,'k');grid on
subplot(2,3,3)
plot(1./P,1./S,'b');grid on
subplot(2,3,4)
plot(1./Q,1./S,'c');grid on
subplot(2,3,5)
plot(teta,Q,'m');grid on
subplot(2,3,6)
```

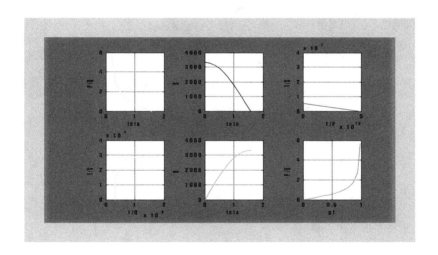

```
del=-2*pi:pi/18:2*pi;
z=sin(del)./del;
plot(del,z,'b');grid on
subplot(2,2,1)
plot(sin(del),z,'k');grid on
subplot(2,2,2)
plot(cos(del),z,'r');grid on
```

```
subplot(2,2,3)
plot(del,1./z,'g');grid on
subplot(2,2,4)
```

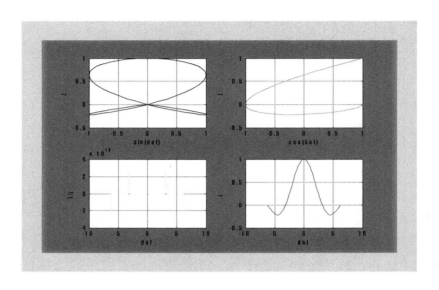

```
del=-2*pi:pi/18:2*pi;
z=sin(del)./del;
plot(del,z,'b');grid on
subplot(2,2,1)
plot(cos(del),cos(z),'k');grid on
subplot(2,2,2)
plot(cos(del),z,'r');grid on
subplot(2,2,3)
plot(del,1./z,'g');grid on
subplot(2,2,4)
```

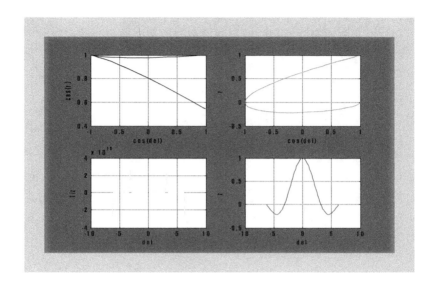

```
s=0:0.1:1;
v=220;r=100;l=0.5;c=100;
i=v./(r+s*l+1./s*c);
plot(s,i,'k');grid on
subplot(2,3,1)
plot(1./s,i,'b');grid on
subplot(2,3,2)
plot(1./s,1./i,'g');grid on
subplot(2,3,3)
plot(i,i.^2,'m');grid on
subplot(2,3,4)
plot(s,s.*i,'r');grid on
subplot(2,3,5)
plot(s,1./i,'c');grid on
subplot(2,3,6)
```

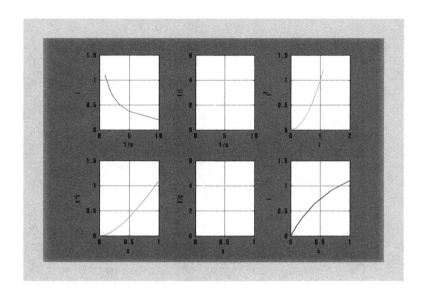

```
s=-1:0.1:1;
v=220;r=100;l=0.5;c=100;
ir=v/r;il=v./(s*l);ic=s*c*v;
plot(1./ic,s./il,'k');grid on
subplot(2,3,1)
plot(s,1./(il+ic),'b');grid on
subplot(2,3,2)
plot(s,(il+ic).^2,'g');grid on
subplot(2,3,3)
plot(1./(il+ic),1./(s.*(il+ic)),'m');grid on
subplot(2,3,4)
plot(s,s./(il+ic),'r');grid on
subplot(2,3,5)
plot(il,1./ic,'c');grid on
subplot(2,3,6)
```

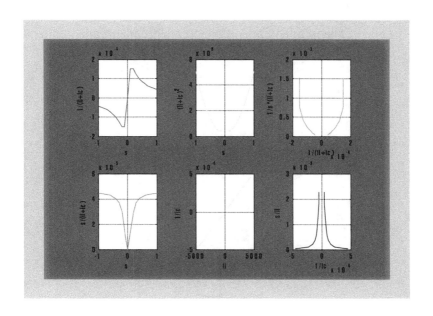

```
s=-1:0.1:1;
r=100;c=100;l=0.5;v=220;
i=v./(r+(l./c./(s.*l+1./s.*c)));
ic=i.*s*l./(s.*l+1./s.*c);
il=i-ic;
plot(ic,i,'k');grid on
subplot(2,3,1)
plot(il,i,'b');grid on
subplot(2,3,2)
plot(s,i,'g');grid on
subplot(2,3,3)
plot(s,il,'r');grid on
subplot(2,3,4)
plot(s,ic,'m');grid on
subplot(2,3,5)
plot(il,ic,'c');grid on
```

subplot(2,3,6)

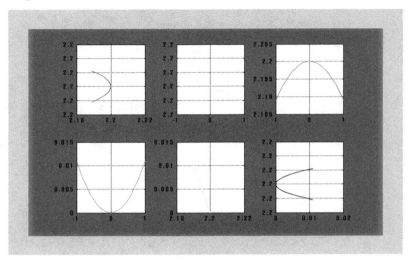

```
beta=-2*pi:pi/18:2*pi;
f=sin(beta)+cos(beta);
plot(f,1./f,'k');grid on
subplot(2,2,1)
plot(beta,f,'r');grid on
subplot(2,2,2)
plot(beta,1./f,'g');grid on
subplot(2,2,3)
plot((beta),f.^2,'m');grid on
subplot(2,2,4)
```

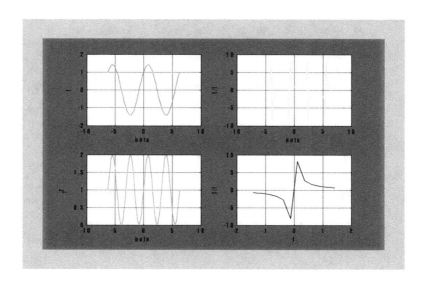

```
beta=-2*pi:pi/18:2*pi;
f=sin(beta)+cos(beta);
plot(f,1./f,'k');grid on
subplot(2,2,1)
plot(beta,f,'r');grid on
subplot(2,2,2)
plot(beta,1./f,'g');grid on
subplot(2,2,3)
plot(sin(beta),f.^2,'m');grid on
subplot(2,2,4)
```

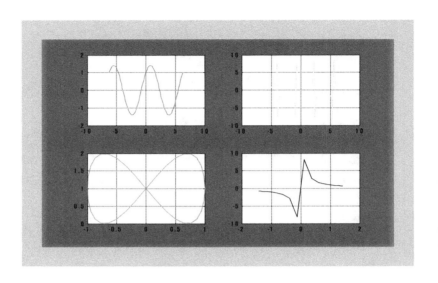

```
beta=-2*pi:pi/18:2*pi;
f=sin(beta)+cos(beta);
plot(f,1./f,'k');grid on
subplot(2,2,1)
plot(beta,f,'r');grid on
subplot(2,2,2)
plot(beta,1./f,'g');grid on
subplot(2,2,3)
plot(cos(beta),f.^2,'m');grid on
subplot(2,2,4)
```

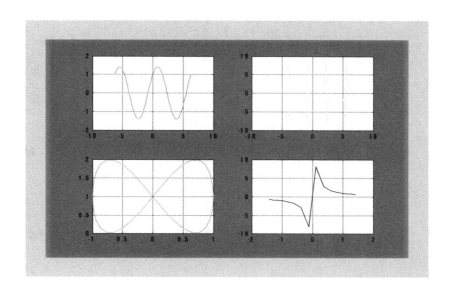

```
beta=-2*pi:pi/18:2*pi;
f=sin(beta)+cos(beta);
plot(f,1./f,'k');grid on
subplot(2,2,1)
plot(beta,f,'r');grid on
subplot(2,2,2)
plot(beta,1./f,'g');grid on
subplot(2,2,3)
plot(cos(beta),sin(f).^2,'m');grid on
subplot(2,2,4)
```

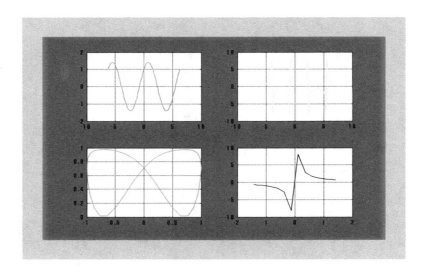

```
beta=-2*pi:pi/18:2*pi;
f=sin(beta)+cos(beta);
plot(f,1./f,'k');grid on
subplot(2,2,1)
plot(beta,f,'r');grid on
subplot(2,2,2)
plot(beta,1./f,'g');grid on
subplot(2,2,3)
plot((beta),tan(f).^2,'m');grid on
subplot(2,2,4)
```

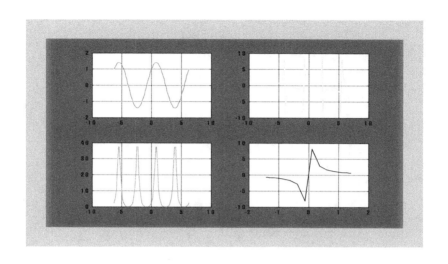

```
beta=-2*pi:pi/18:2*pi;
f=sin(beta)+cos(beta);
plot(f,1./f,'k');grid on
subplot(2,2,1)
plot(beta,f,'r');grid on
subplot(2,2,2)
plot(beta,1./f,'g');grid on
subplot(2,2,3)
plot(sin(beta),sin(f),'m');grid on
subplot(2,2,4)
```

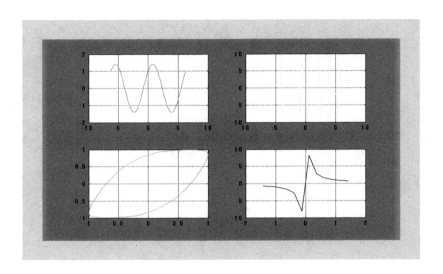

```
beta=-2*pi:pi/18:2*pi;
f=sin(2*beta)+cos(beta);
plot(f,1./f,'k');grid on
subplot(2,2,1)
plot(beta,f,'r');grid on
subplot(2,2,2)
plot(beta,1./f,'g');grid on
subplot(2,2,3)
plot(sin(beta),sin(f),'m');grid on
subplot(2,2,4)
```

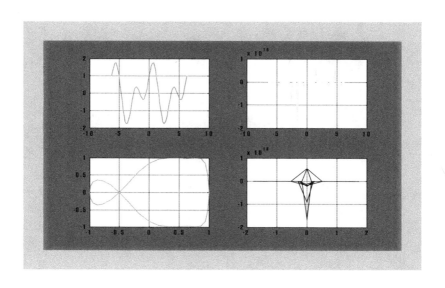

```
beta=-2*pi:pi/18:2*pi;
f=sin(2*beta)+cos(2*beta);
plot(f,1./f,'k');grid on
subplot(2,2,1)
plot(beta,f,'r');grid on
subplot(2,2,2)
plot(beta,1./f,'g');grid on
subplot(2,2,3)
plot(sin(beta),sin(f),'m');grid on
subplot(2,2,4)
```

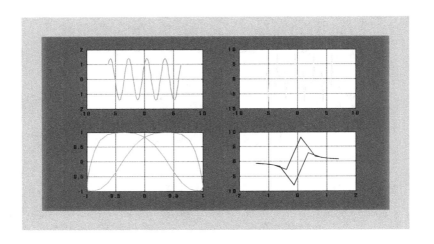

```
beta=-2*pi:pi/18:2*pi;
f=sin(3*beta)+cos(2*beta);
plot(f,1./f,'k');grid on
subplot(2,2,1)
plot(beta,f,'r');grid on
subplot(2,2,2)
plot(beta,1./f,'g');grid on
subplot(2,2,3)
plot(sin(beta),sin(f),'m');grid on
subplot(2,2,4)
```

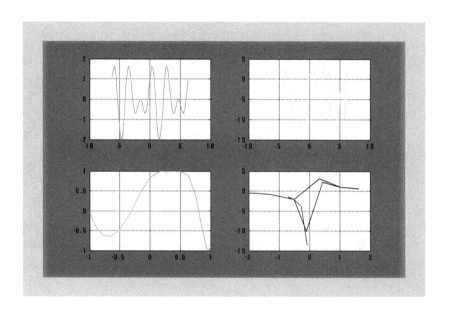

```
beta=-2*pi:pi/18:2*pi;
f=sin(2*beta)+cos(3*beta);
plot(f,1./f,'k');grid on
subplot(2,2,1)
plot(beta,f,'r');grid on
subplot(2,2,2)
plot(beta,1./f,'g');grid on
subplot(2,2,3)
plot(sin(beta),sin(f),'m');grid on
subplot(2,2,4)
```

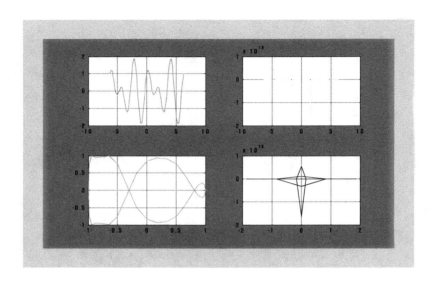

```
x=[-10:2:10];
y=x.^3;
plot(x,y,'c');grid on
subplot(2,2,1)
plot(x,1./y,'g');grid on
subplot(2,2,2)
plot(1./x,1./y,'m');grid on
subplot(2,2,3)
plot(x.^2,y.^2,'r');grid on
subplot(2,2,4)
```

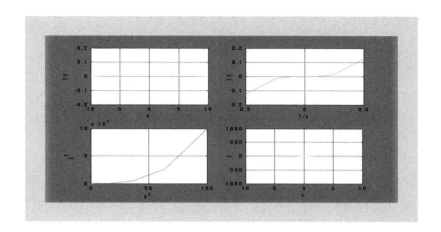

CHAPTER 17

17.0 TRANSFER FUNCTION IN CONTROL SYSTEM

```
s=-1:0.1:1;
G=(s+2).*(s+4)./(s+1).*(s+3).*(s+5);
H=1;
V=1+G*H;
plot(s,G,'r');grid on
subplot(2,2,1)
plot(G,V,'m');grid on
subplot(2,2,2)
plot(s,V,'c');grid on
subplot(2,2,3)
plot(s,G./V,'g');grid on
subplot(2,2,4)
```

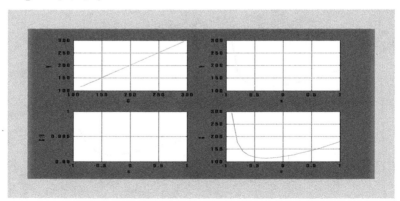

264

```
x=-10:2:10;
y=x.^2+4.*x+4;
z=1./y;
w=1./x;
plot(x,y,'r');grid on
subplot(2,2,1)
plot(x,z,'g');grid on
subplot(2,2,2)
plot(y,z,'c');grid on
subplot(2,2,3)
plot(w,z,'m');grid on
subplot(2,2,4)
```

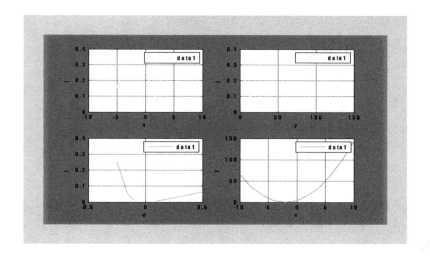

Insert

Click on a particular figure and then insert to label the axes. For figures that involve more than one, click on a particular figure and then insert. The command will choose at random when a particular figure is not click before the insert command is used.

Edit

You can use this command to copy the figure to be pasted.

Tools

The plot could be edited using the tool bar. This will enable the user to insert the label at appropriate position.

Plot(x,y,'r')grid on

This command plots the graph of x against y using red color with grid lines.

18.0 LOGIC OPERATIONS

OR LOGIC OPERATION

This is achieved by entering the inputs separated by the logic operation command. The logic operation command is selected by *'shift key and back slash key'*.

A	B	C
0	0	0
0	1	1
1	0	1
1	1	1

The above 'or' truth table is realized using MATLAB as follows

>> 0|0

ans =

    0

>> 0|1

ans =

  1

>> 1|0

ans =

  1

>> 1|1

ans =

  1

A	B	C	D
0	0	0	0
0	0	1	1
0	1	0	1
0	1	1	1
1	0	0	1
1	0	1	1
1	1	0	1
1	1	1	1

The above 'or' truth table is realized using
MATLAB as follows

```
>> 0|0|0

ans =

    0

>> 0|0|1

ans =

    1

>> 0|1|0

ans =

    1
```

```
>> 0|1|1

ans =

    1

>> 1|0|0

ans =

    1

>> 1|0|1

ans =

    1
```

```
>> 1|1|0

ans =

    1

>> 1|1|1

ans =

    1
```

AND LOGIC OPERATION

This is achieved by entering the inputs separated by the logic operation command. The logic operation command is selected by *'shift key and 7'.*

A	B	C
0	0	0
0	1	0
1	0	0
1	1	1

The above 'and' truth table is realized using matlab as follows

>> 0&0

ans =

    0

>> 0&1

ans =

0

>> 1&0

ans =

0

>> 1&1
ans =
1

A	B	C	D
0	0	0	0
0	0	1	0
0	1	0	0
0	1	1	0
1	0	0	0
1	0	1	0
1	1	0	0
1	1	1	1

The above 'or' truth table is realized using MATLAB as follows

```
>> 0&0&0


ans =



    0



>> 0&0&1

ans =

    0
```

```
>> 0&1&0

ans =

    0

>> 0&1&1
ans =


    0


>> 1&0&0

ans =

    0


>> 1&0&1
ans =

    0
```

>> 1&1&0

ans =

   0

>> 1&1&1

ans =

   1

NOT LOGIC OPERATION

This is achieved by entering operation command then the number. The operation command is obtained by *'shift key and .'*.

A	B
0	1
1	0

The above 'NOT' truth table is realized using matlab as follows

>> ~1

ans =

   0

>> ~0

ans =

   1

EXCLUSIVE OR LOGIC OPERATION

This is achieved by entering operation command then the numbers separated by comma in bracket. The operation command is 'xor'.

A	B	C
0	0	0
0	1	1
1	0	1
1	1	0

The above 'EXCLUSIVE OR' truth table is realized using MATLAB as follows

```
>> xor(0,0)

ans =

    0

>> xor(0,1)


ans =

    1


>> xor(1,0)

ans =

    1


>> xor(1,1)
```

ans =

   0

NAND LOGIC OPERATION

This is achieved by entering 'AND' logic operation in bracket with 'NOT' logic command in front of the bracket.

A	B	C
0	0	1
0	1	1
1	0	1
1	1	0

The above 'NAND' truth table is realized using MATLAB as follows

>> ~(0&0)

ans =

   1

>> ~(0&1)

ans =

1

>> ~(1&0)

ans =

1

>> ~(1&1)

ans =

0

NOR LOGIC OPERATION

This is achieved by entering 'OR' logic operation in bracket with 'NOT' logic command in front of the bracket.

A	B	C
0	0	1
0	1	0
1	0	0
1	1	0

The above 'NOR' truth table is realized using MATLAB as follows

\>\> ~(0|0)

ans =

   1

\>\> ~(0|1)

ans =

   0

\>\> ~(1|0)

ans =

   0

\>\> ~(1|1)

ans =

   0

CHAPTER 18

18.0 TO DETERMINE INVERSE LAPLACE TRANSFORM.

Question

Find inverse Laplace of 1/(s+1)

Solution

>> syms s;

>> ilaplace(1/(s+1))

ans =

exp(-t)

e^{-t}

Question

Determine the inverse laplace transform of

$$\frac{1}{S+2}$$

Solution

>> syms s

>> ilaplace (1/(s+2))

ans =

exp(-2*t)

e^{-2t}

Question

Find inverse Laplace transform of 100/ (s²+100)

Solution

>> syms s;

>> ilaplace(100/(s^2+100))

ans =

10*sin(10*t)

Question

Find the inverse laplace transform of

$$\frac{10}{S^2 + 5S + 6}$$

Solution

\>> syms s

\>> ilaplace(10/(s^2+5*s+6))

ans =

10*exp(-2*t) - 10*exp(-3*t)

$10e^{-2t} - 10e^{-3t}$

TO DETERMINE LAPLACE TRANSFORM

Question

Find the Laplace transform of sin (t)

Solution

>> syms t;

>> laplace(sin(t))

ans =

1/(s^2+1)

$$\frac{1}{s^2 + 1}$$

Question

Find the laplace transform of

$$t^2$$

Solution

>> syms t

>> laplace(t^2)

ans =

2/s^3

$$\frac{2}{s^3}$$

Question

Find the Laplace transform of

$$t^2 + 4t + 4$$

Solution

>> syms t

>> laplace(t^2+4*t+4)

ans =

4/s + 4/s^2 + 2/s^3

$$\frac{4}{s} + \frac{4}{s^2} + \frac{2}{s^3}$$

Question

Find the Laplace transform of

$$t + \cos(t) + \sin(2t)$$

Solution

>> syms t

>> laplace(t+cos(t)+sin(2*t))

ans =

s/(s^2 + 1) + 2/(s^2 + 4) + 1/s^2

$$\frac{S}{S^2 + 1} + \frac{2}{S^2 + 4} + \frac{1}{S^2}$$

Question

Find the laplace transform of

$$t^3 + \sin(2t) - \cos(3t)$$

Solution

>> syms t

>> laplace(t^3+sin(2*t)-cos(3*t))

ans =

2/(s^2 + 4) - s/(s^2 + 9) + 6/s^4

$$\frac{2}{S^2 + 4} - \frac{S}{S^2 + 9} + \frac{6}{S^4}$$

CHAPTER 19

18.0 APPLICATION OF SIMULINK

The Simulink is activated by double clicking on the *Simulink library* icon on the MATLAB platform.

Accessing Simulink

Step 1

Double click on Simulink box on top of MATLAB platform

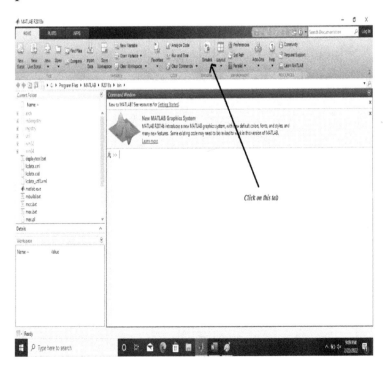

288

Step 2

Double click on the first box tagged *Blank Model*

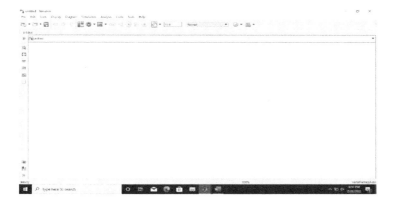

289

Step3

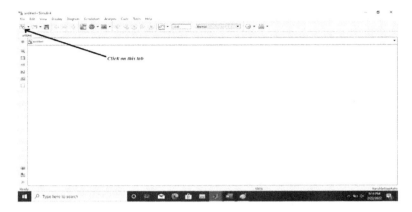

Step 4

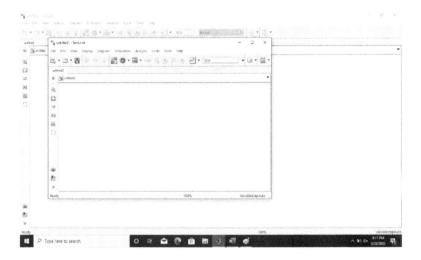

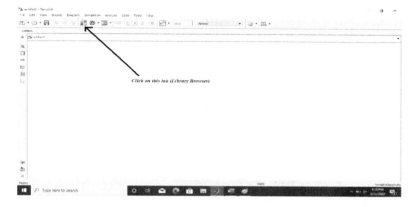

Click on this tab (Library Browser)

Step 5

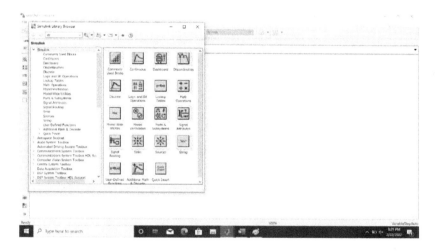

The block diagram of figure 25.0 depicts the steps taken to assess the various blocks needed for the simulation.

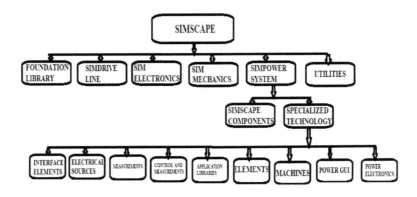

Figure 25.0 Block diagram for the steps utilized on Simulink.

Example

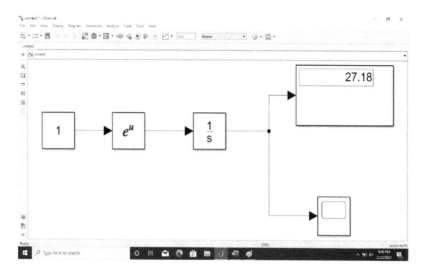

Scope Result

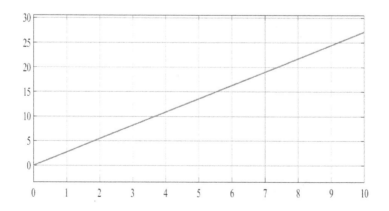

293

Example 2

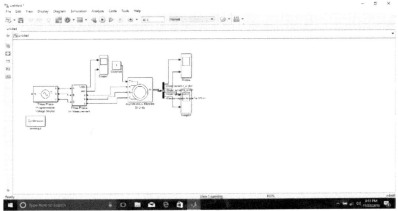

Figure 25.1 Simulink blocks arrangement with scopes

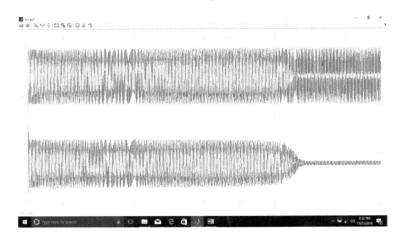

Figure 25.2 Waveform for the input supply

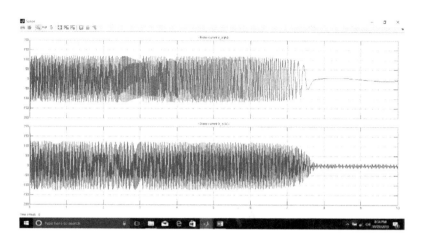

Figure 25.2 Waveform for the stator and rotor voltages

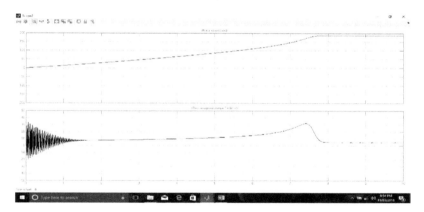

Figure 25.3. The rotor speed and electromagnetic torque for the asynchronous motor.

Example 2

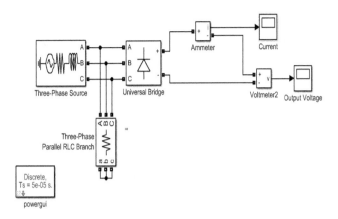

Figure 25.4 Simulink blocks for full wave rectification of three-phase supply.

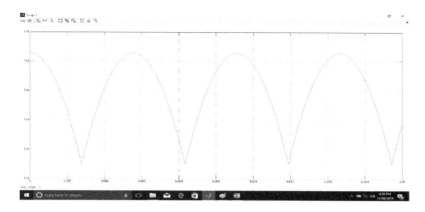

Figure 25.5 Voltage waveform

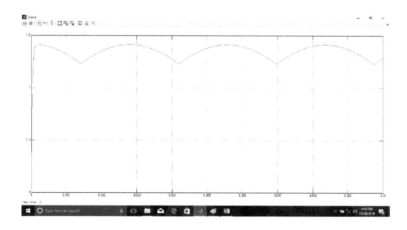

Figure 25.6 Current waveform

297

Example 3

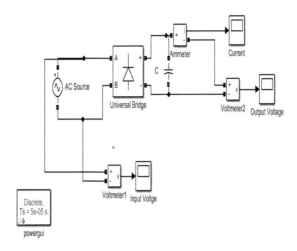

Figure 25.7 (a) Simulink Diagram of Full Wave
Rectifier with Smoothing Capacitor.

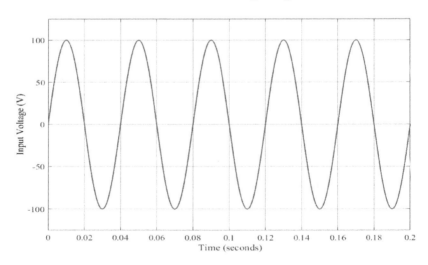

Figure 25.7 (b) Input Voltage Waveform

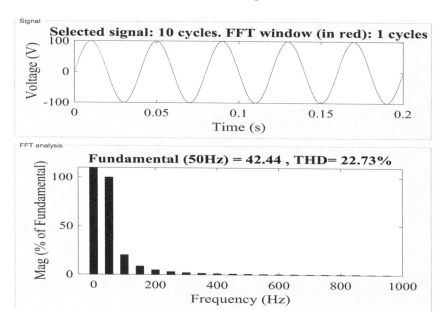

Figure 25.7 (c) FFT for the Input Voltage Waveform

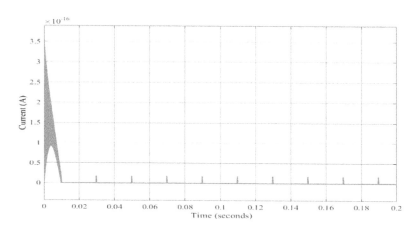

Figure 25.7 (d) Current Waveform

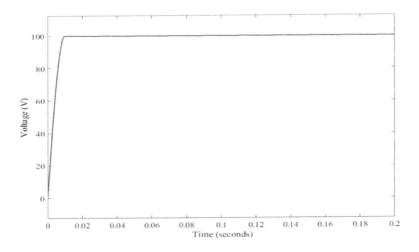

Figure 25.7 (e) Output Voltage Waveform

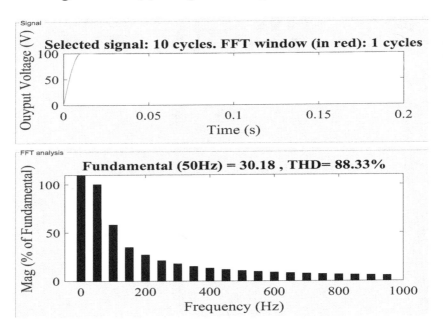

Figure 25.7 (f) FFT of the Output Voltage
Waveform

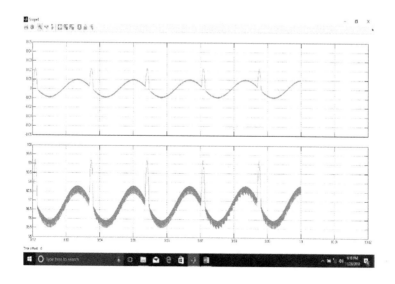

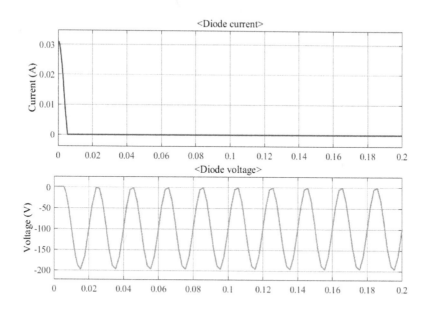

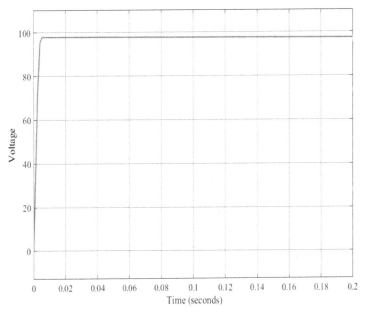

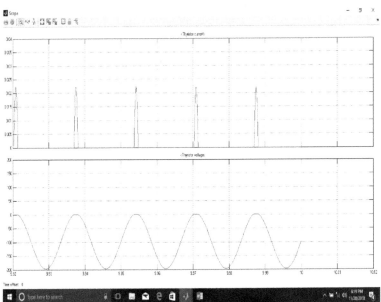

Example 3

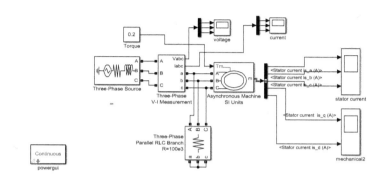

Figure 25.8 (a) Simulink Diagram for Three-Phase Induction Motor

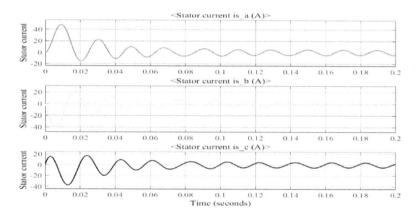

Figure 25.8 (b) Stator Current Waveforms

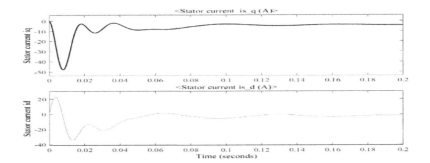

Figure 25.8 (c) Stator Direct Axis Current
Waveform

Example 4

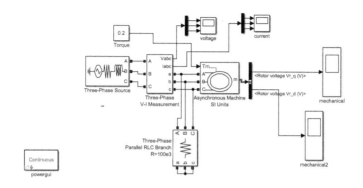

Figure 25.9 (a) Simulink Diagram

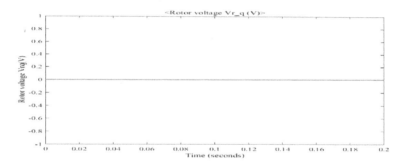

Figure 25.9 (b) Rotor Waveform

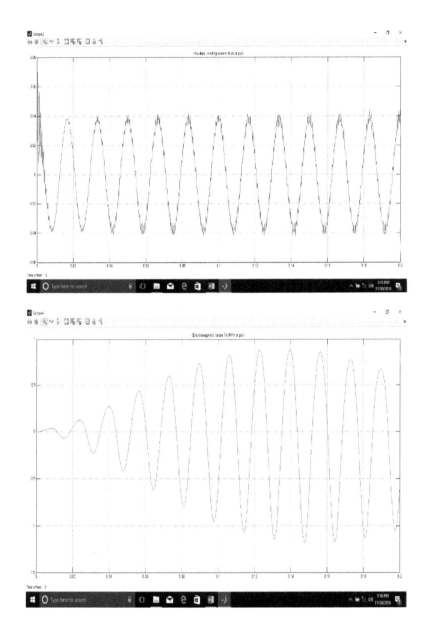

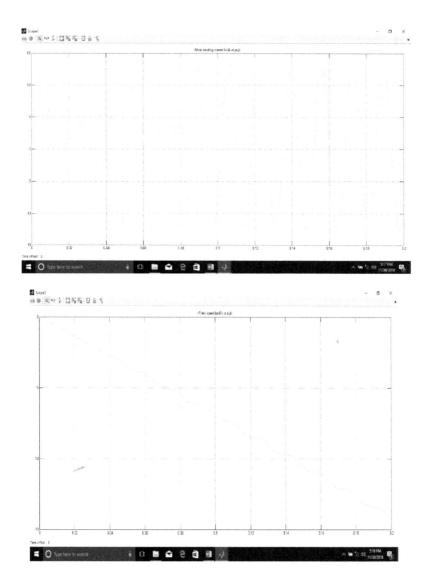

Example 5

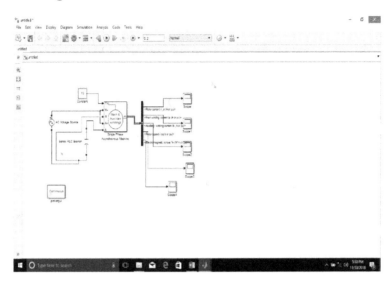

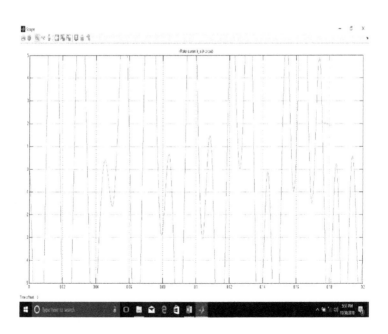

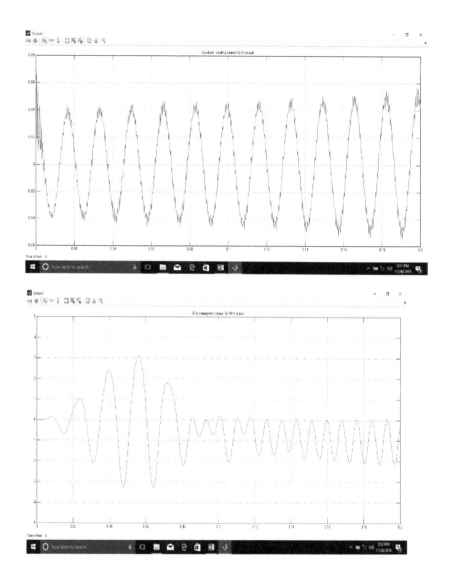

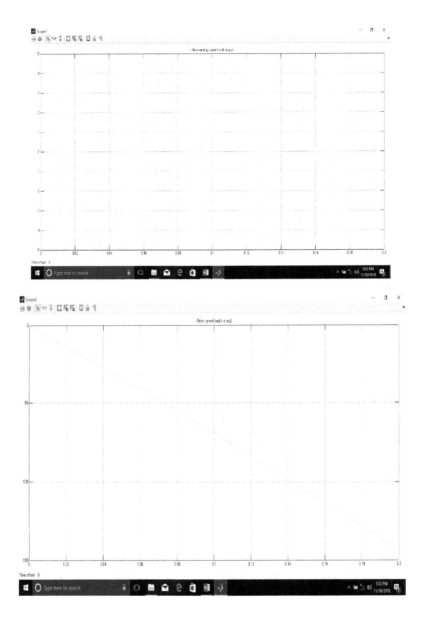

Example 6

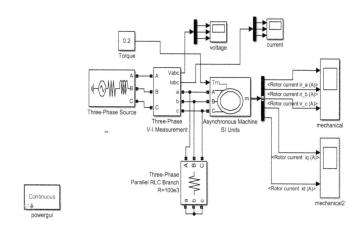

Figure 26.0 (a) Simulink Diagram

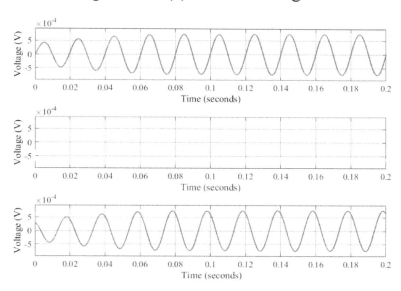

Figure 26.0 (b) Voltage Waveform

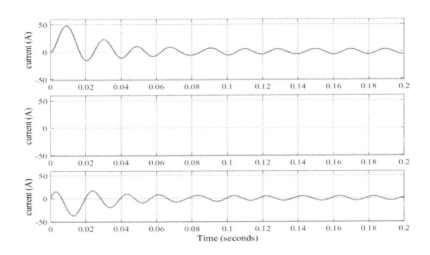

Figure 26.0 (c) Current Waveform

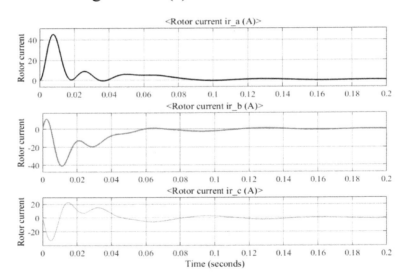

Figure 26.0 (d) Rotor Current Waveform

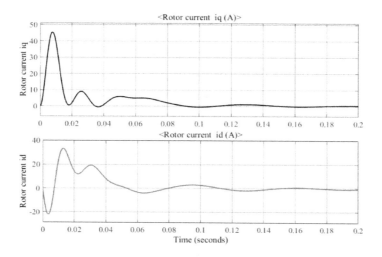

Figure 26.0 (e) Rotor Current Waveform

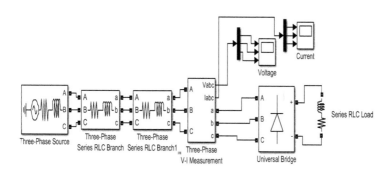

Figure 27.0 (a) Simulink diagram

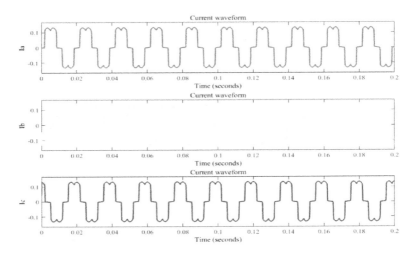

Figure 27.0 (b) Current waveform

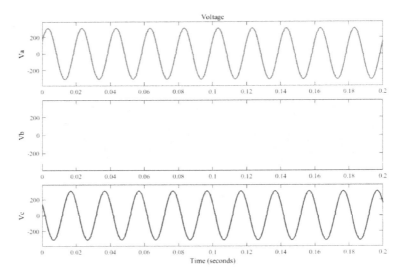

Figure 27.0 (c) Voltage waveform

314

Steps taken in getting the FFT analysis to indicate the level of Total Harmonic Distortions.

Step 1 Click on the setting on the graph platform

Step 2 Scroll to logging, then click log data to workspace

Step 3 Click on power-guide and scroll to the FFT

Step 4 Ensure the information as displayed on the platform is the same with the actual one on the graph platform.

Step 5 Click on DISPLAY under the page.

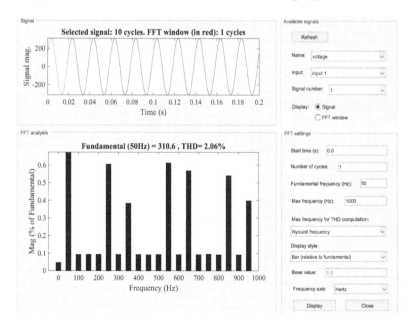

Figure 27.0 (d) Voltage FFT analysis graph

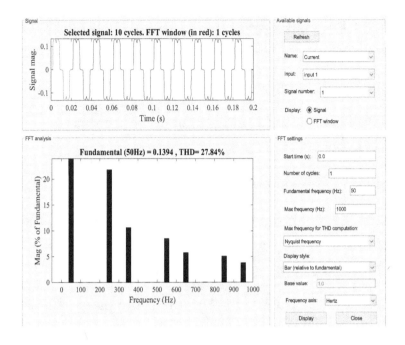

Figure 27.0 (e) Current FFT analysis graph

The figure 28.0 (a) depicts the Simulink diagram of three-phase supply to an induction motor (asynchronous machine).

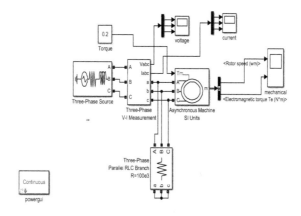

Figure 28.0 (a) Simulink diagram for the three-phase supply to an induction motor.

The various waveforms as indicated on the scopes are as shown in figures 28.0 (b) to (d).

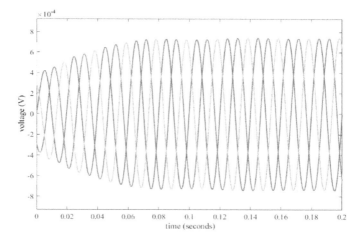

Figure 28.0 (b) Voltage waveform

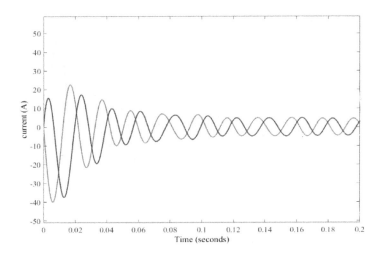

Figure 28.0 (c) Current waveform

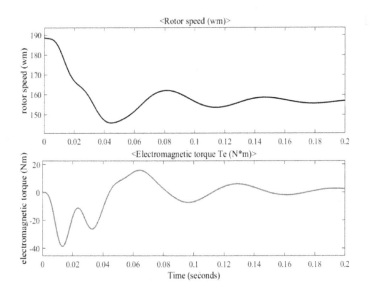

Figure 28.0 (d) mechanical waveforms

318

The **FFT analysis** is obtained by clicking on the **configuration properties** by the top left-hand side of the displayed graph. Then select **logging**. Scroll down to **log data to work space** and select.

It is important to check the level of Harmonic Distortions in the system. This is realized by clicking on the **power-Gui**. Then select **Tools**. Scroll to the **FFT analysis box**. Click on this box. The display of the platform is as shown in figure 29. Then change the parameters that are suitable to your design. Under the box tagged **Name**, the list of graphs that are available on the Simulink are displayed. Press **Display** at the bottom of the platform to display the THD chart. Select one after the other to determine the respective THD levels.

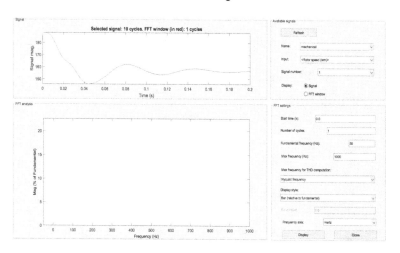

Figure 29.0 FFT analysis platform

319

The FFT analysis for the current is as shown in figure 29.0 (a).

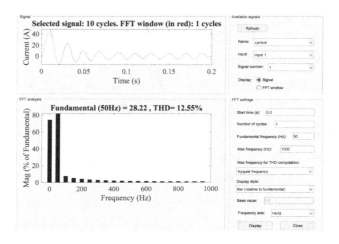

Figure 29.0 (a) Current waveform indicating the THD level

The FFT analysis for the voltage is as shown in figure 29.0 (b).

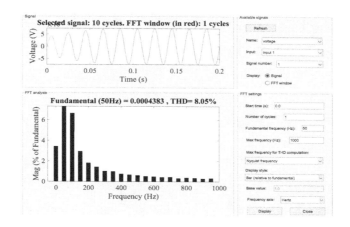

Figure 29.0 (b) Voltage waveform indicating
the THD level

The FFT analysis for the rotor speed is as shown in
figure 29.0 (c).

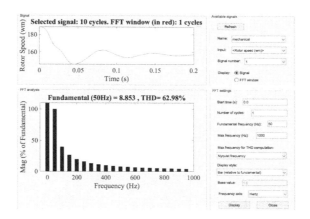

Figure 29.0 (c) Rotor speed waveform
indicating the THD level

321

The FFT analysis for the electromagnetic torque is as shown in figure 29.0 (d).

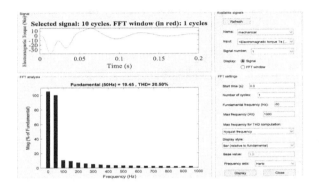

Figure 29.0 (d) Electromagnetic torque indicating the THD level

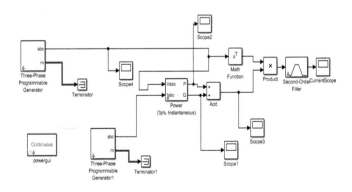

Figure 30 (a) Simulink diagram

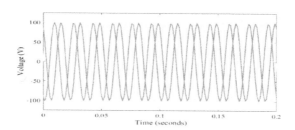

Figure 30.0 (b) Voltage Waveform

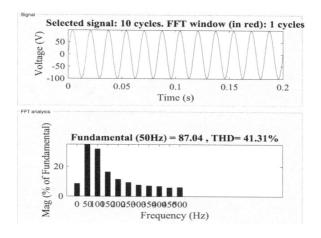

Figure 30.0 (c) FFT for the Voltage
Waveform

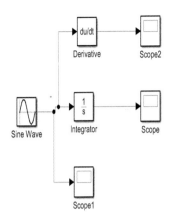

Figure 31.0 (a) Simulink Diagrams to demonstrate Output Responses.

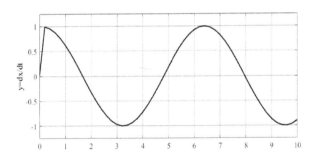

Figure 31 (b) Output response from the differentiator.

324

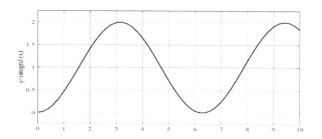

Figure 31.0 (c) Output Response from the integrator

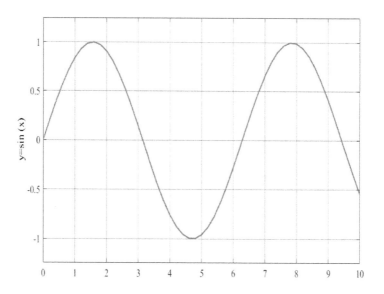

Figure 31.0 (d) Output response for the sinusoidal Waveform.

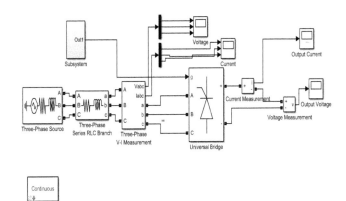

Figure 32.0 (a) Simulink Diagram for Controlled Rectifier

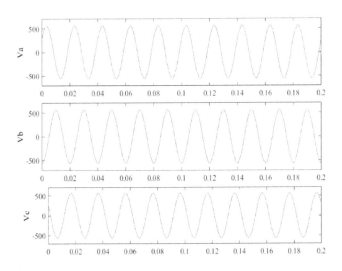

Figure 32 (b) Voltage Waveform

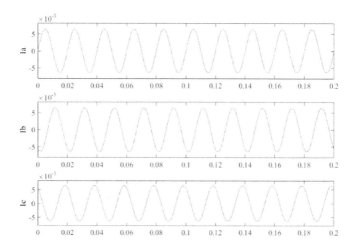

Figure 32 (c) Current Waveform

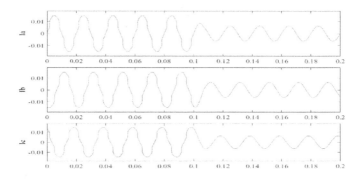

Figure 32.0 (d) Output Current Waveform

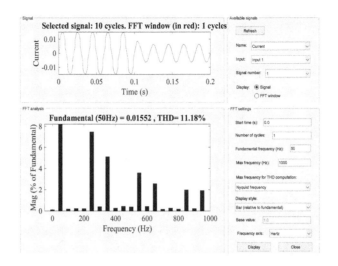

Figure 32 (e) FFT for the Output Current

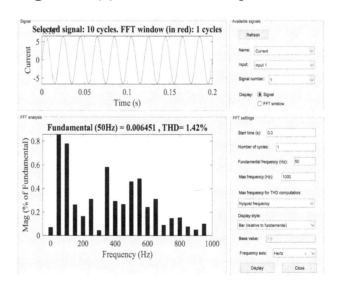

Figure 32.0 (f) FFT for the Voltage
Waveform

www.ingramcontent.com/pod-product-compliance
Lightning Source LLC
LaVergne TN
LVHW051430050326
832903LV00030BD/3015